LIVING THE WISDOM OF SOLOMON

PART I

KNOWLEDGE UNDERSTANDING WISDOM

JOHN W. PRIDE

Living the Wisdom of Solomon
Part I: Knowledge, Understanding, Wisdom

05 04 03 02 01 10 9 8 7 6 5 4 3 2 1

ISBN: 0-9794586-1-7
Copyright © 2007 by John W. Pride

Published by: John W. Pride
Tulsa, Oklahoma

To order additional copies contact:
John W. Pride
Post Office Box 702002
Tulsa, Oklahoma 74170-2002
Phone: 918-841-2867 Fax: 918-524-9292
Website: www.johnwpride.com
Email: johnwpride@cox.net

Dedication

First, I would like to dedicate this book to our Heavenly Father, who inspired and instructed me to write it for the benefit of His children, the Body of Christ.

Secondly, I want to thank and express my appreciation to my wonderful wife, Cindy and our two children, Madison and Jonathan, for their prayers, support and encouragement.

Thirdly, I want to dedicate this book to YOU, the member of the Body of Christ who is reading it. For it is for you that this book was written. I trust you will benefit from it greatly. As your Knowledge, Understanding and Wisdom increase, I believe that your life will be blessed, as well as the Body of Christ as a whole. I pray now that God will reveal His Knowledge, Understanding and Wisdom to you as you read, study and mediate on His Word and pray. God bless you immensely!

John W. Pride

Author's Note

The title of this book was going to be "Almost... As Wise As Solomon" First, this book is about the Knowledge, Understanding and Wisdom the book of Proverbs teaches us about most of which Solomon wrote. I first thought of making the title "As Wise As Solomon," however, I could not since God told Solomon in I Kings 3:12 "Behold, I have done as you asked. I have given you a wise, discerning mind, so that no one before you was your equal, nor shall any arise after you equal to you." Amp. No one will ever be as wise as Solomon, however, we can be... "Almost As Wise As Solomon." With God's wisdom and living a Holy Spirit-led life we can have tremendous success in all areas of our life. We can begin... "Living the Wisdom of Solomon."

Introduction

Proverbs is one of my favorite books of the Bible. It has so much practical advice for all areas of our lives. As I have read Proverbs throughout the years, I noticed one thing that made it difficult to thoroughly understand and that is it jumps from one subject to another frequently throughout the book.

As I was reading, studying and meditating on some of these proverbs, I felt it would be so much easier to understand if they were grouped together by subject, put into an order that would be easier to understand and explained in words we use today. God put on my heart and instructed me to do this for the Body of Christ.

Once I began, I found this was going to be a huge undertaking. I quickly learned there are 915 verses in Proverbs. However, I chose to be obedient to what God instructed me to do. My first task was to separate the 915 verses into subjects, which I have done. There are 385 subjects.

I felt God wanted me to write about Knowledge, Understanding and Wisdom first. After much studying and meditating on these verses, this book contains all of the verses in Proverbs that pertain to these three subjects, sorted and resorted with explanations for each verse. There are 37 verses that pertain to Knowledge, 42 verses that pertain to Understanding and 193 verses pertaining to Wisdom.

I felt it would aid in understanding if I also included three commonly read translations of the Bible for each of these verses, so I have chosen the *King James*, *Amplified* and *New International Versions*, listed side by side, with an explanation next to them.

Sorting into chapters and sub-chapters provided an outline that created an overview. This seems to help in seeing the overall picture, especially after you have read this book.

I am excited for you to begin reading, studying and meditating on God's Word as you read this book. God is ready to reveal His Knowledge, Understanding and Wisdom to you! So get ready to become . . . . Almost . . . . As Wise As Solomon!

Suggestions While Reading and Studying This Book

1. The three subjects contained in this book were put into the order of <u>Knowledge first</u>, <u>Understanding second</u> and <u>Wisdom third</u> on purpose, signifying the order in which a person obtains them.

2. Try to <u>grasp concepts</u> and to see "the whole picture" of how Knowledge, Understanding and Wisdom fit together, keeping a key fact in mind, there are certain things that <u>we must do</u> to obtain them.

3. Learn and understand <u>how you will use</u> Knowledge, Understanding and Wisdom in your daily life, <u>in every decision you make</u>.

4. Learn and understand <u>how you will greatly benefit in every area of your life</u>; i.e., finances, family, work, relationships, self, etc. This will be the <u>motivating factor that will drive you to do what is required of you</u>.

5. Be determined not to just read this book, but to <u>put into practice what you will learn</u>. God wants you to be wise as much as you do!

6. Begin to <u>see yourself</u> having <u>the characteristics of wisdom</u>.

7. Begin <u>doing</u> what <u>Wisdom instructs you to do</u>.

8. Begin <u>reading, studying and meditating on God's Word and praying</u>.

9. Begin expecting <u>new ideas</u> to "pop" into your mind. Pray about the decisions you have to make and <u>ask God for discretion to make the wisest decisions</u>.

10. <u>Expect</u> to <u>obtain Knowledge</u>, for <u>Understanding</u> to be <u>revealed to you by God</u> and for <u>you to become Wiser</u>.

11. <u>Read, study and meditate on the "Explanations" from beginning to end</u> for they have been assembled into an order to <u>make understanding easier</u>, using the three translations as references and study aids.

12. <u>Study and understand</u> the <u>Key Definitions</u> before beginning to read the rest of the book.

KEY DEFINITIONS

Discernment or Discerning:
> the ability to sense what is not evident to other people

Discipline:
> to train by instruction and control

Discretion:
> the ability to make responsible decisions

Folly:
> lack of good sense or normal prudence and foresight; i.e., evil, wickedness

Fools:
> a person lacking in sound judgment or prudence, lacks understanding

Insight:
> (or discernment) – the ability to see into a situation

Instruction:
> the action or practice of teaching. A direction calling for compliance

Mockers:
> to treat with contempt or ridicule, insulting action or speech

Prudent:
> skill, good judgment and common sense

Reprove:

>to scold or correct usually gently or with kindly intent; to express disapproval of; a kindly intent to correct a fault

Scorner:

>one who rejects or dismisses as contemptible (act of despising, lack of respect or reverence for something) or unworthy. Open dislike or disrespect

Simple:

>being or seeming unable to use sound judgment, discretion, or good sense (one without moral direction and inclined to evil)

Wisdom:

>ability to discern inner qualities and relationships. Knowledge; Insight; Good Sense; Judgment; a wise attitude or course of action

I. KNOWLEDGE

A. God Uses Knowledge to . . .   19

B. The Purpose of Having Knowledge   19
   1. To Be Able to Give Sound or Correct Answers

C. What Is the Source of Knowledge?   21
   1. God's Word and the Holy Spirit

D. What's Required to Obtain Knowledge   21
   1. The Fear or Reverence of the Lord

   2. What We Must Do To Find the Knowledge
     of God

   3. Knowledge Comes Easily to Those
     with Discernment

   4. Prudent People Desire to Obtain Knowledge

   5. Accept Corrective Criticism Positively
     and Gain More Knowledge

   6. Commit to Accept Instruction
     and Listen to Words of Knowledge

E. Knowledge is Valuable   26
   1. Obtaining Knowledge Is More Valuable than
     Financial Gain

   2. Wise People Value Knowledge

3. Being Able to Speak the Knowledge Is Very Rare

F. Having Knowledge Will Protect You   27
  1. Delivered, Rescued and Escape Destruction
  2. God Will Preserve or Keep Knowledge

G. Knowledge Causes Us to Understand
   Wisdom's Teachings   29

H. Your Words Will Reflect Your Knowledge   31

I. Knowledge and Discipline   33

J. Wise People Value Knowledge Greatly   33

K. What Having Knowledge Will Do for You   35

L. Fools Hate Knowledge   37

II. UNDERSTANDING

A. God Is the Source of Understanding   41

B. What's Required to Obtain Understanding   46

C. Characteristics of Having Understanding   55

D. The Rewards of Having Understanding   59

E. Foolish People "Can" Obtain Understanding
   If They Do What Is Required   66

III. WISDOM

A. The Beginning of Wisdom   71
1. God Created Wisdom
2. God Used Wisdom
3. Wisdom Brought God Great Joy
4. Respect and Honor the Lord is Where
We Begin

B. The Purpose of Having Wisdom   77
1. So We Can Know What Is "Right"
2. Wisdom Is Used By Many People

C. Who Can Have Wisdom?   79
1. Wisdom Is Available to Everyone

D. How to Get Wisdom   81
1. What is the Beginning of Wisdom?
2. We Must Humble Ourselves Before God
3. How Important Is It To Get Wisdom?
4. Where Do We Get Wisdom?
5. What We Must Do To Get Wisdom
6. Wisdom is Easily Understood By Those
Who Have Obtained Knowledge and Understanding
7. We Are to Concentrate on Understanding
Wisdom's Teachings
8. We Are to Love and Cherish Wisdom
and Understanding
9. Wisdom Loves Us If We Love Wisdom

10. We Must Humble Ourselves and Listen to Advice of Wise People

11. Wise People Listen to Other Wise People to Become Even Wiser

12. Blessed Are Those People Who Do as Wisdom Instructs

E. Characteristics of Having Wisdom   89

  1. Righteous, Upright, Good and Obedient

  2. Wins Souls

  3. Lives a Godly Lifestyle

  4. Stores Up Knowledge

  5. Speaks Uplifting Words to Others

  6. Speaks Kind Words

  7. Distributes Knowledge with His Words

  8. Is Greatly Valued By Someone Who Received and Obeyed Correction

  9. Willing to Listen to Advice

10. Gives Wise Advice and Speaks Words of Wisdom

11. Capable of Giving Good Advice and Making Sound Judgment or Decisions

12. Has Discernment Whether Advice Is Good or Bad

13. Thinks Before He Speaks & Chooses His Words Wisely

14. Listens to Constructive Criticism

15. Remains Quiet When He Could Respond in Defense or Retaliation

16. Controls His Anger

17. Turns Away Anger

18. Thinks About and Knows What To Do Before Doing It

19. Wise Plans

20. Has Understanding

21. Works Hard

22. Wealth

23. Favor of Those in Authority Over You

24. A Wise Woman Develops Her Family and Home

25. Spanks and Corrects Their Children and Speaks Kind Words to Them

26. A Wise Son Listens Carefully to His Father

27. Makes Parents Proud

28. Overcomes Disadvantages

29. Has Self-Discipline and Initiative

30. Determined

31. Chooses Not to Be Around Sin, Wickedness, Bad Character or Conduct

32. Opposes the Wicked

33. Hates Wickedness

34. Strengthened By Using Wisdom Consistently

35. Uses Wisdom Daily

36. Gets Satisfaction or Gratification By Having and Using Wisdom

37. Keeps His Focus and Attention on Wisdom

F. Wisdom's Instruction to Us   119

1. Reverence God

2. Humble Ourselves

3. Meditate Upon Wisdom's Instruction

4. Listen to Wisdom and Do as Instructed

5. Wise Action

6. Hang Around Wise People

7. Work

8. Be Fair in Judging

9. Children

10. Make Your Parents Proud

11. Do Not Attempt to Teach Fools Wisdom's Ways

G. What Having Wisdom Will Do for You   128

1. What We Must Do

2. Safety and Peace

3. Happiness, Joy and Peace

4. Protection

5. Our Thoughts and Emotions Will Be Pleasant

6. Your Mind and Emotions Will Benefit

7. Life and Health to Your Body, Mind and Soul

8. Long Life, Riches and Honor

9. Praise, Honor and Distinction

10. You Will Be Successful, Promoted, Honored, Prosperous and Wise

11. Dignity and Honor By Others

12. You Will Be Complimented and Praised

13. Strength

14. Your Parents Will Be Proud of You

15. God Will Be on Your Side

16. Life and Favor of God

17. Promotion, Financial Blessing and Favor of Men

18. Riches, Honor, Enduring Wealth and Righteousness

19. Choose Wisdom Rather Than Money

20. Wisdom Is the Most Valuable

21. Wisdom Is More Valuable Than Money

22. Prudence and Financial Blessings

23. Ability to Make Wise Decisions

24. Life Made Easier

25. You Will Benefit in All Areas of Life

H. What Happens If Someone Rejects Wisdom?   147

1. Wisdom Will Not Be Available When
They Need It

2. They Will Suffer the Consequences

3. They Will Make Their Parents Sad and Disappointed

4. It Will Bring Shame Upon Them

5. It Will Cause Their Family To Be Divided

6. Their Foolish Words Will Bring Them Punishment

7. Leads to a Very Costly Undertaking

8. It Will Cost Them Financially

9. They Will Become a Servant to the Wise

10. They Will Suffer Ruin, Defeat and Failure

11. Destruction Will Come Upon Them

I. Characteristics of Not Having Wisdom   157

1. Refuses to Accept Wisdom

2. Fools Hate Wisdom and Discipline

3. Ignores Wisdom and Has No Desire to
Have Knowledge

4. Reasons Why Some People Do Not Have Wisdom

5. He Has No Desire to Get Wisdom

6. Fools Will Not Listen to Others

7. They Will Not Listen When Rebuked

8. Resents Someone Correcting Him

9. Displays Violent and Uncontrollable Anger

10. Speaks Words That Are Absurd, Ridiculous and Based on Poor Judgment

11. Speaks Destructive Words

12. His Words Do Not Distribute Knowledge

13. Excuses

14. Spends All of His Money as He Gets It

15. Is Deceived of the Effects Alcohol Has on Them

16. Does Not Like Their Mother

17. They Can Learn to Become Wiser

Conclusion   169

Testimony   171

I

KNOWLEDGE

A. God Uses Knowledge to...

NIV 3:20   by his knowledge the deeps are divided, and the clouds let drop the dew.

KJV 3:20   By his knowledge the depths are broken up, and the clouds drop down the dew.

AMP 3:20   By His knowledge the deeps were broken up, and the skies distill the dew.

God used His "knowledge" to create the oceans and the rain. He "knew" what man needed on earth to survive. Knowledge has always been used by God, even from the beginning of the earth. God wants us to have knowledge. We must do our part and study His Word and listen to His voice through the Holy Spirit.

B. The Purpose of Having Knowledge

NIV 1:4   for giving prudence to the simple, knowledge and discretion to the young.

KJV 1:4   To give subtilty to the simple, to the young man knowledge and discretion.

AMP 1:4   That prudence may be given to the simple, and knowledge, discretion, and discernment to the youth–

The proverbs of Solomon were given to provide prudence to the simple and knowledge and discretion to young people. Prudence is skill, good judgment and common sense. The simple are people who do not use sound judgment, discretion or good sense. The purpose of the proverbs is to provide people who do not use sound judgment, discretion or good sense with the skill, good judgment and common sense they need to be successful in all areas of life. Knowledge, or the truth and facts of life that a person acquires either through experience or thought and discretion, or the ability to make responsible decisions, are to be gained by people, preferably when they are young, as knowledge and discretion will serve them well throughout their lives.

1. To Be Able to Give Sound or Correct Answers

NIV 22:20-21 Have I not written thirty sayings for you, sayings of counsel and knowledge, teaching you true and reliable words, so that you can give sound answers to him who sent you?

KJV 22:20-21 Have not I written to thee excellent things in counsels and knowledge, that I might make thee know the certainty of the words of truth; that thou mightest answer the words of truth to them that send unto thee?

AMP 22:20-21 Have I not written to you [long ago] excellent things in counsels and knowledge, to make you know the certainty of the words of truth, that you may give a true answer to those who sent you?

The purpose of gaining knowledge is to be able to give sound or correct answers.

C. What Is the Source of Knowledge?

1. God's Word and the Holy Spirit

NIV 2:6   For the LORD gives wisdom, and from his mouth come knowledge and understanding.

KJV 2:6   For the LORD giveth wisdom: out of his mouth cometh knowledge and understanding.

AMP 2:6   For the Lord gives skillful and godly Wisdom; from His mouth come knowledge and understanding.

Wisdom comes from God. From his "mouth" comes knowledge and understanding. What is God's "mouth"? God's Word, the Bible, is God's mouth. We gain divine knowledge and understanding by studying and meditating on God's Word. God can also speak to us through the Holy Spirit. As we hear what He is speaking to us through the Holy Spirit, we gain wisdom. As we do, God gives us wisdom.

D. What's Required to Obtain Knowledge?

1. The Fear or Reverence of the Lord

NIV 1:7   The fear of the LORD is the beginning of knowledge, but fools despise wisdom and discipline.

KJV 1:7   The fear of the LORD is the beginning of knowledge: but fools despise wisdom and instruction.

AMP 1:7   The reverent and worshipful fear of the Lord is the beginning and the principal and choice part of knowledge [its starting point and its essence]; but fools despise skillful and godly Wisdom, instruction, and discipline.

The first and most fundamental principle for obtaining wisdom is the "fear" or reverence of the Lord. No real knowledge of God's truth can be obtained unless God's love is supreme in one's heart. Foolish people hate wisdom and instruction (or discipline). They are the ones who have a careless attitude towards life. Discipline, or to train by instruction and control, is not part of their lifestyle.

Proverbs 9:10

NIV 9:10   The fear of the LORD is the beginning of wisdom, and knowledge of the Holy One is understanding.

KJV 9:10   The fear of the LORD is the beginning of wisdom: and the knowledge of the holy is understanding.

AMP 9:10   The reverent and worshipful fear of the Lord is the beginning (the chief and choice part) of Wisdom, and the knowledge of the Holy One is insight and understanding.

Before we can obtain wisdom, we must first respect, love, honor and esteem God. Knowledge of God, His grace, His love, His mercy results in understanding for us. God will "reveal" to us through His Holy Spirit as we seek Him first.

2. What We Must Do To Find the Knowledge of God

NIV 2:5   Then you will understand the fear of the LORD and find the knowledge of God.

KJV 2:5   Then shalt thou understand the fear of the LORD, and find the knowledge of God.

AMP 2:5   Then you will understand the reverent and worshipful fear of the Lord and find the knowledge of [our omniscient] God.

There are conditions that we must meet before we will understand the fear or reverence of God and find the knowledge of God. We must: (1) accept wisdom's words, (2) memorize and meditate on wisdom's commands until we understand them, (3) listen to wisdom's teachings, (4) sincerely apply our hearts to understanding, (5) earnestly desire insight and understanding, (6) search for insight and understanding relentlessly, THEN we will understand the fear or reverence of the Lord and find the knowledge of God.

Proverbs 2:10

NIV 2:10   For wisdom will enter your heart, and knowledge will be pleasant to your soul.

KJV 2:10   When wisdom entereth into thine heart, and knowledge is pleasant unto thy soul;

AMP 2:10   For skillful and godly Wisdom shall enter into your heart, and knowledge shall be pleasant to you.

As we study God's Word and pray, we must: (1) accept wisdom's words, (2) memorize and meditate to thoroughly understand, and (3) search for insight and understanding. THEN, we will understand the fear and respect of God and find the knowledge of God.

The knowledge of God will bring you joy and happiness.

3. Knowledge Comes Easily to Those with Discernment

NIV 14:6   The mocker seeks wisdom and finds none, but knowledge comes easily to the discerning.

KJV 14:6   A scorner seeketh wisdom, and findeth it not: but knowledge is easy unto him that understandeth.

AMP 14:6   A scoffer seeks Wisdom in vain [for his very attitude blinds and deafens him to it], but knowledge is easy to him who [being teachable] understands.

A person who treats others with ridicule, insults and makes fun of them, cannot obtain wisdom when he looks for it, but the person who has the ability to sense what is not evident to other people obtains knowledge easily.

4. Prudent People Desire to Obtain Knowledge

NIV 18:15   The heart of the discerning acquires knowledge; the ears of the wise seek it out.

KJV 18:15   The heart of the prudent getteth knowledge; and the ear of the wise seeketh knowledge.

AMP 18:15   The mind of the prudent is ever getting knowledge, and the ear of the wise is ever seeking (inquiring for and craving) knowledge.

The person with good judgment and common sense obtains knowledge, while the wise person listens carefully, seeking to find more knowledge.

5. Accept Corrective Criticism Positively and Gain More Knowledge

NIV 19:25   Flog a mocker, and the simple will learn prudence; rebuke a discerning man, and he will gain knowledge.

KJV 19:25   Smite a scorner, and the simple will beware: and reprove one that hath understanding, and he will understand knowledge.

AMP 19:25   Strike a scoffer, and the simple will learn prudence; reprove a man of understanding, and he will increase in knowledge.

If a person who ridicules, insults and makes fun of others is criticized harshly, people who have been unable to use good judgment or common sense will learn to use good judgment and common sense. If a person who has the ability to sense what is not evident to other people is criticized sharply, he will take it positively and gain more knowledge from it.

6. Commit to Accept Instruction and Listen to Words of Knowledge

NIV 23:12   Apply your heart to instruction and your ears to words of knowledge.

KJV 23:12   Apply thine heart unto instruction, and thine ears to the words of knowledge.

AMP 23:12   Apply your mind to instruction and correction

and your ears to words of knowledge.

The way we become knowledgeable is to commit our undivided attention to being taught or instructed, with a humble attitude and to be sensitive to recognize words that make us more knowledgeable.

E. Knowledge Is Valuable

1. Obtaining Knowledge Is More Valuable Than Financial Gain

NIV 8:10   Choose my instruction instead of silver, knowledge rather than choice gold,

KJV 8:10   Receive my instruction, and not silver; and knowledge rather than choice gold,

AMP 8:10   Receive my instruction in preference to [striving for] silver, and knowledge rather than choice gold,

Obtaining wisdom's instruction and knowledge are more "valuable" than gold, silver, rubies or anything else you desire. Gaining knowledge and increasing in wisdom should be what we value, as opposed to the materialistic things. If we "seek ye first" wisdom and knowledge, God will bless us with wealth anyway.

2. Wise People Value Knowledge

NIV 10:14 Wise men store up knowledge, but the mouth of a fool invites ruin.

KJV 10:14   Wise men lay up knowledge: but the mouth of the foolish is near destruction.

AMP 10:14   Wise men store up knowledge [in mind and heart], but the mouth of the foolish is a present destruction.

Wise people realize the value of knowledge and they study to gain it. However, the words a foolish person (someone who lacks good sense or prudence) speaks cause him trouble and eventually ruin.

3. Being Able to Speak the Knowledge Is Very Rare

NIV 20:15   Gold there is, and rubies in abundance, but lips that speak knowledge are a rare jewel.

KJV 20:15   There is gold, and a multitude of rubies: but the lips of knowledge are a precious jewel.

AMP 20:15   There is gold, and a multitude of pearls, but the lips of knowledge are a vase of preciousness [the most precious of all].

Obtaining knowledge is one thing, but to be able to speak the knowledge we have is extremely uncommon. Knowing and understanding well enough to speak the knowledge is very valuable to the one who speaks it as well as to the ones who hear it.

F. Having Knowledge Will Protect You

1. Delivered, Rescued and Escape Destruction

NIV 11:9   With his mouth the godless destroys his

neighbor, but through knowledge the righteous escape.

KJV 11:9   An hypocrite with his mouth destroyeth his neighbour: but through knowledge shall the just be delivered.

AMP 11:9   With his mouth the godless man destroys his neighbor, but through knowledge and superior discernment shall the righteous be delivered.

The godless or hypocrite destroys friendships with their evil words. Through knowledge and wise discernment, the godly, the righteous, the just, are delivered, rescued and escape destruction.

2. God Will Preserve or Keep Knowledge

NIV 22:12   The eyes of the LORD keep watch over knowledge, but he frustrates the words of the unfaithful.

KJV 22:12   The eyes of the LORD preserve knowledge, and he overthroweth the words of the transgressor.

AMP 22:12   The eyes of the Lord keep guard over knowledge and him who has it, but He overthrows the words of the treacherous.

God will preserve or keep knowledge; however, he will ruin the plans of the deceitful. God will protect us if we are putting Him first and He will give us the desires of our hearts.

G. Knowledge Causes Us to Understand Wisdom's Teachings

NIV 8:9   To the discerning all of them are right; they are faultless to those who have knowledge.

KJV 8:9   They are all plain to him that understandeth, and right to them that find knowledge.

AMP 8:9   They are all plain to him who understands [and opens his heart], and right to those who find knowledge [and live by it].

All the words of wisdom and understanding are "right" to those who have discernment (the ability to sense what is not evident to the average person). To those who have knowledge, the teachings of wisdom and understanding are perfect and clearly understood.

Proverbs 8:12

NIV 8:12   I, wisdom, dwell together with prudence; I possess knowledge and discretion.

KJV 8:12   I wisdom dwell with prudence, and find out knowledge of witty inventions.

AMP 8:12   I, Wisdom [from God], make prudence my dwelling, and I find out knowledge and discretion.

Someone who has wisdom will also have prudence, which is having good judgment and common sense. If a person has wisdom, they also have knowledge and discretion, the ability to make responsible decisions.

Proverbs 24:4

NIV 24:4   through knowledge its rooms are filled with rare and beautiful treasures.

KJV 24:4   And by knowledge shall the chambers be filled with all precious and pleasant riches.

AMP 24:4   And by knowledge shall its chambers [of every area] be filled with all precious and pleasant riches.

The analogy of a house being built is used here, with wisdom "building" the house, understanding "establishing" the house and knowledge "filling" its rooms with rare and beautiful treasures. We are the "house." As someone increases in wisdom, it is a "building" process, little by little, adding more wisdom day by day, as God gives it. As this is occurring, we are to do our part in studying God's Word to gain knowledge and for God to be able to give us understanding. As these occur simultaneously, the "house" (being a wise, knowledgeable, mature Christian with lots of understanding) is complete, strong, rare and beautiful.

Proverbs 24:5

NIV 24:5   A wise man has great power, and a man of knowledge increases strength;

KJV 24:5   A wise man is strong; yea, a man of knowledge increaseth strength.

AMP 24:5   A wise man is strong and is better than a strong man, and a man of knowledge increases and strengthens his power.

When a person becomes wise, he or she becomes "powerful" in many different areas. As their knowledge increases so does their "strength." As 23:12 states, we must be teachable and willing to listen to sound advice. As we do, we become wiser and more knowledgeable, always being humble and ready to gain more wisdom and knowledge. As one does this, while another does not do this, it will become evident that the one who pursued wisdom will be much wiser and much more knowledgeable than the person who did not. Many times, the person who did not seek wisdom and knowledge is the person who goes about their daily routine, without even putting forth any effort in praying, studying God's Word or doing something for the kingdom of God.

H. Your Words Will Reflect Your Knowledge

NIV 5:2   that you may maintain discretion and your lips may preserve knowledge.

KJV 5:2   That thou mayest regard discretion, and that thy lips may keep knowledge.

AMP 5:2   That you may exercise proper discrimination and discretion and your lips may guard and keep knowledge and the wise answer [to temptation].

We must carefully and intently listen to wisdom's teachings and her words of insight (or discernment) in order for us to be able to continue being discreet (the ability to make responsible decisions) so that the words we speak will continue to be words spoken from the knowledge we have gained.

NIV 17:27   A man of knowledge uses words with restraint, and a man of understanding is even-
tempered.

KJV 17:27   He that hath knowledge spareth his words:
and a man of understanding is of an excellent
spirit.

AMP 17:27   He who has knowledge spares his words, and a
man of understanding has a cool spirit.

A wise person who has obtained knowledge thinks before he
speaks and then is selective in what he says. A person who has
understanding does not get angry easily.

Proverbs 20:15

NIV 20:15   Gold there is, and rubies in abundance, but
lips that speak knowledge are a rare jewel.

KJV 20:15   There is gold, and a multitude of rubies: but
the lips of knowledge are a precious jewel.

AMP 20:15   There is gold, and a multitude of pearls, but
the lips of knowledge are a vase of preciousness
[the most precious of all].

Obtaining knowledge is one thing, but to be able to speak
the knowledge we have is extremely uncommon. Knowing and
understanding well enough to speak the knowledge is very valuable to the one who speaks it as well as to the ones who hear it.

I. Knowledge and Discipline

NIV 12:1   Whoever loves discipline loves knowledge, but he who hates correction is stupid.

KJV 12:1   Whoso loveth instruction loveth knowledge: but he that hateth reproof is brutish.

AMP 12:1   Whoever loves instruction and correction loves knowledge, but he who hates reproof is like a brute beast, stupid and indiscriminating.

The word translated "instruction" here refers to discipline or correction. The person who loves discipline (to be trained by instruction and control) also loves knowledge and will use discipline in gaining knowledge. He who hates to be corrected and gets angry is showing little intelligence.

J. Wise People Value Knowledge Greatly

NIV 15:2   The tongue of the wise commends knowledge, but the mouth of the fool gushes folly.

KJV 15:2   The tongue of the wise useth knowledge aright: but the mouth of fools poureth out foolishness.

AMP 15:2   The tongue of the wise utters knowledge rightly, but the mouth of the [self-confident] fool pours out folly.

The words of the wise person embrace or praise knowledge. Knowledge is valued greatly by wise people. However, the person who lacks good judgment and common sense speaks mostly foolishness.

Proverbs 15:14

NIV 15:14 The discerning heart seeks knowledge, but the mouth of a fool feeds on folly.

KJV 15:14 The heart of him that hath understanding seeketh knowledge: but the mouth of fools feedeth on foolishness.

AMP 15:14 The mind of him who has understanding seeks knowledge and inquires after and craves it, but the mouth of the [self-confident] fool feeds on folly.

The wise person wants more and more knowledge, realizing how important it is.

Proverbs 21:11

NIV 21:11 When a mocker is punished, the simple gain wisdom; when a wise man is instructed, he gets knowledge.

KJV 21:11 When the scorner is punished, the simple is made wise: and when the wise is instructed, he receiveth knowledge.

AMP 21:11 When the scoffer is punished, the fool gets a lesson in being wise; but men of [godly] Wisdom and good sense learn by being instructed.

When a person who ridicules or insults another is punished, the person who is unable to use sound judgment, discretion or good sense, gains wisdom or learns. When a wise person is instructed or taught, he is willing to listen and learn and he gets knowledge.

K. What Having Knowledge Will Do for You

NIV 13:16 Every prudent man acts out of knowledge, but a fool exposes his folly.

KJV 13:16 Every prudent man dealeth with knowledge: but a fool layeth open his folly.

AMP 13:16 Every prudent man deals with knowledge, but a [self-confident] fool exposes and flaunts his folly.

Every person who uses good judgment and common sense does so because he has knowledge, but a person who lacks good sense or prudence is seen by others as foolish.

Proverbs 19:2

NIV 19:2 It is not good to have zeal without knowledge, nor to be hasty and miss the way.

KJV 19:2 Also, that the soul be without knowledge, it is not good; and he that hasteth with his feet sinneth.

AMP 19:2 Desire without knowledge is not good, and to be overhasty is to sin and miss the mark.

If a person pursues something with eagerness and great interest without having the knowledge he needs, mistakes will surely be made which will create problems and cause heart-ache and great loss. Nor is it wise to make quick decisions and make mistakes.

Proverbs 24:5

NIV 24:5   A wise man has great power, and a man of knowledge increases strength;

KJV 24:5   A wise man is strong; yea, a man of knowledge increaseth strength.

AMP 24:5   A wise man is strong and is better than a strong man, and a man of knowledge increases and strengthens his power.

When a person becomes wise, he or she becomes "powerful" in many different areas. As their knowledge increases so does their "strength." As 23:12 states, we must be teachable and willing to listen to sound advice. As we do, we become wiser and more knowledgeable, always being humble and ready to gain more wisdom and knowledge. As one does this, while another does not do this, it will become evident that the one who pursued wisdom will be much wiser and much more knowledgeable than the person who did not. Many times, the person who did not seek wisdom and knowledge is the person who goes about their daily routine, without even putting forth any effort in praying, studying God's Word or doing something for the kingdom of God.

Proverbs 28:2

NIV 28:2   When a country is rebellious, it has many rulers, but a man of understanding and knowledge maintains order.

KJV 28:2   For the transgression of a land many are the princes thereof: but by a man of understanding and knowledge the state thereof shall be prolonged.

AMP 28:2　When a land transgresses, it has many rulers, but when the ruler is a man of discernment, understanding, and knowledge, its stability will long continue.

Another analogy, this time concerning "rebellion." Just as the people within a country are rebellious, they will have many "rulers," creating chaos. The same is true within a person. If he or she allows the "things of the world" to dominate their time, attention and thoughts, then they too will have many "rulers." God wants us to put Him first. "A man of understanding and knowledge maintains order." He knows and understands if he puts God first, everything else will fall into place and blessings will abound unto him.

L. Fools Hate Knowledge

NIV 1:22　How long will you simple ones love your simple ways? How long will mockers delight in mockery and fools hate knowledge?

KJV 1:22　How long, ye simple ones, will ye love simplicity? and the scorners delight in their scorning, and fools hate knowledge?

AMP 1:22　How long, O simple ones [open to evil], will you love being simple? And the scoffers delight in scoffing and [self-confident] fools hate knowledge?

Wisdom looks at the simple, the scornful and the foolish with disapproval and distrust. "Simple" people are people who are not using good judgment, discretion or good sense. The "scornful" or mockers treat others with contempt or ridicule, insulting action or speech. The "foolish" ignores the instruction of wisdom and despises wisdom and discipline. He mocks (ridicules) guilt and is quarrelsome (argues a lot). These people do not want to be "bothered" with wisdom. If they are given money, they waste it. If they are hired, they miss out on promotions. If they are offered a free education, they will not study. They waste their time and poorly clothe and house themselves. Nothing could be further from their minds than wisdom.

Proverbs 1:29

NIV 1:29   Since they hated knowledge and did not choose to fear the LORD.

KJV 1:29   For that they hated knowledge, and did not choose the fear of the LORD.

AMP 1:29   Because they hated knowledge and did not choose the reverent and worshipful fear of the Lord.

Wisdom gives two reasons why the time comes when she can no longer be found. The first is that she has been hated: "They hated knowledge, and did not choose to fear (or love and respect) the Lord." The hate and the choice are linked together. People hate wisdom because wisdom cannot be separated from the fear (or love and respect) of the Lord, and the fear (or love and respect) of the Lord is the last thing to appeal to the unrepentant, stubborn human heart. Many people want no part of any wisdom that directs their thoughts to God.

Proverbs 14:7

NIV 14:7   Stay away from a foolish man, for you will not find knowledge on his lips.

KJV 14:7   Go from the presence of a foolish man, when thou perceivest not in him the lips of knowledge.

AMP 14:7 Go from the presence of a foolish and self-confident man, for you will not find knowledge on
his lips.

Stay away from a foolish person, someone who lacks good
judgment and common sense, because you will not find knowledge from his words and actions. Instead, his ideas and words
will be foolish and he will try to convince you he is correct
when in fact he is incorrect.

Proverbs 15:14

NIV 15:14 The discerning heart seeks knowledge, but
the mouth of a fool feeds on folly.

KJV 15:14 The heart of him that hath understanding
seeketh knowledge: but the mouth of fools
feedeth on foolishness.

AMP 15:14 The mind of him who has understanding
seeks knowledge and inquires after and craves
it, but the mouth of the [self-confident] fool
feeds on folly.

The person who is wise and discerning does what is required
of him to obtain knowledge. The foolish person, lacking good
judgment and common sense, spends his time on things that do
him no good.

Proverbs 19:27

NIV 19:27 Stop listening to instruction, my son, and you
will stray from the words of knowledge.

KJV 19:27 Cease, my son, to hear the instruction that
causeth to err from the words of knowledge.

AMP 19:27   Cease, my son, to hear instruction only
to ignore it and stray from the words of
knowledge.

If a person who used to listen to wisdom's instruction stops listening to wisdom's instruction, he will stop following what knowledge he had obtained. His actions and words will no longer be wise, but foolish instead.

II

UNDERSTANDING

A. God Is the Source of Understanding

NIV 2:6   For the LORD gives wisdom, and from his mouth come knowledge and understanding.

KJV 2:6   For the LORD giveth wisdom: out of his mouth cometh knowledge and understanding.

AMP 2:6   For the Lord gives skillful and godly Wisdom; from His mouth come knowledge and understanding.

For the Lord gives us wisdom. The source of wisdom is God. Therefore, we must ask God to give us wisdom. Then we must do our part to study to allow God to reveal His knowledge to us until we obtain a thorough, complete understanding, such that we can speak the knowledge that God has revealed to us to other people who have not yet received such knowledge, to inspire them to also strive to obtain God's knowledge. And from the Lord's mouth come knowledge and understanding. God speaks to us through His Word, the Bible, and through the Holy Spirit.

In order for us to obtain this knowledge and understanding, we must study (not just read) God's Word (the Bible) and meditate upon it day and night until we thoroughly understand it. But, do not get overwhelmed as many people do, trying to read and understand the Bible in its entirety. Instead, study certain subjects at a time, from various translations and God will reveal to you the meaning of His Word and help you to understand. As we do, God will reveal certain truths to us concerning our lives and how we are to live our lives.

Likewise, God speaks to us through His Holy Spirit. When Jesus rose from the dead and went to Heaven, God sent us "another Comforter," the Holy Spirit, who can live inside each one of us. However, we must choose to accept or receive this gift and then we must learn to be sensitive to "hear" what the Holy Spirit has to tell us, not in an audible voice, but by thoughts coming into our mind. By yielding to the Holy Spirit, we can "tap into" God's divine knowledge and understanding. We communicate by speaking and listening. When we "speak" or pray in the Holy Spirit, we speak in tongues, a prayer language that God has for us that if we choose to receive it, allows us to more freely hear what God has to "say" to us through His Holy Spirit.

Proverbs 3:19

NIV 3:19   By wisdom the LORD laid the earth's foundations, by understanding he set the heavens in place;

KJV 3:19   The LORD by wisdom hath founded the earth; by understanding hath he established the heavens.

AMP 3:19   The Lord by skillful and godly Wisdom has founded the earth; by understanding He has established the heavens.

God used His "understanding" to set the heavens in place and His wisdom to lay the earth's foundations. God's wisdom and understanding, which can be ours, are extremely powerful!

Proverbs 4:1

NIV 4:1   Listen, my sons, to a father's instruction; pay attention and gain understanding.

KJV 4:1   Hear, ye children, the instruction of a father, and attend to know understanding.

AMP 4:1   Hear, my sons, the instruction of a father, and pay attention in order to gain and to know intelligent discernment, comprehension, and interpretation [of spiritual matters].

Children "gain" understanding by listening closely to their father's (and mother's) instruction or teaching. A child is born without any understanding. A father or mother has lived many more years and has learned and can teach a child much he or she does not know. Likewise, our Heavenly Father will teach us what we do not know. We can gain understanding by listening closely to our Heavenly Father's instruction or teaching, through studying His Word and praying and listening to Him.

Proverbs 8:1-9

NIV 8:1-9 Does not wisdom call out? Does not understanding raise her voice? On the heights along the way, where the paths meet, she takes her stand; beside the gates leading into the city, at the entrances, she cries aloud: "To you, O men, I call out; I raise my voice to all mankind. You who are simple, gain prudence; you who are foolish, gain understanding. Listen, for I have worthy things to say; I open my lips to speak what is right. My mouth speaks what is true, for my lips detest wickedness. All the words of my mouth are just; none of them is crooked or perverse. To the discerning all of them are right; they are faultless to those who have knowledge.

KJV 8:1-9 Doth not wisdom cry? and understanding put forth her voice? She standeth in the top of high places, by the way in the places of the paths. She crieth at the gates, at the entry of the city, at the coming in at the doors. Unto you, O men, I call; and my voice is to the sons of man. O ye simple, understand wisdom: and, ye fools, be ye of an understanding heart. Hear; for I will speak of excellent things; and the opening of my lips shall be right things. For my mouth shall speak truth; and wickedness is an abomination to my lips. All the words of my mouth are in righteousness; there is nothing froward or perverse in them. They are all plain to him that understandeth, and right to them that find knowledge.

AMP 8:1-9 Does not skillful and godly Wisdom cry out, and understanding raise her voice [in contrast to the loose woman]? On the top of the heights beside the way, where the paths meet, stands Wisdom [skillful and godly]; at the gates at the entrance of the town, at the coming in at the doors, she cries out: To you, O men, I call, and my voice is directed to the sons of men. O you simple and thoughtless ones, understand prudence; you [self-confident] fools, be of an understanding heart.

Hear, for I will speak excellent and princely things; and the opening of my lips shall be for right things. For my mouth shall utter truth, and wrongdoing is detestable and loathsome to my lips. All the words of my mouth are righteous (upright and in right standing with God); there is nothing contrary to truth or crooked in them. They are all plain to him who understands [and opens his heart], and right to those who find knowledge [and live by it].

In these nine verses, it is evident that wisdom and understanding are trying to get our attention and stress to us how important it is for all people to listen and understand what they have to say. "Simple" people are those who seem or are unable to use good judgment, discretion or common sense. They are instructed to "gain prudence." "Prudence" is having good judgment or common sense.

Notice, people who do not have good judgment or common sense can change and "gain" prudence. Likewise, foolish people (foolish and simple are synonyms, having similar meanings), are instructed to "gain understanding." There is hope for foolish and simple people. However, if they are going to gain or get prudence and understanding, they must humble themselves and choose to do what is required of them and that is to study God's Word, earnestly, with a burning desire to obtain more and more of God's wisdom and understanding. Wisdom and understanding go on to tell us that the things they have for us to learn are "worthy" or very important. What they reveal to us is right, true and just. They detest or hate wickedness. To those people who have discernment, or the ability to sense what is not evident to other people, all of the words of wisdom and understanding are right. The words of wisdom and understanding are easy to understand to those who have the knowledge that God revealed to them. Therefore, seek God in His Word and communicate with Him and allow God to reveal His wisdom, His understanding and His knowledge to you.

Proverbs 24:3

NIV 24:3   By wisdom a house is built, and through understanding it is established;

KJV 24:3   Through wisdom is an house builded; and by understanding it is established:

AMP 24:3   Through skillful and godly Wisdom is a house (a life, a home, a family) built, and by understanding it is established [on a sound and good foundation],

Our bodies are "temples" of the Holy Spirit. As we obtain wisdom, wisdom becomes the foundation for all that we say and do. We become strengthened or more developed, more mature, as we gain understanding through God revealing it to us.

B. What's Required to Obtain Understanding?

NIV 2:2   turning your ear to wisdom and applying your heart to understanding.

KJV 2:2   So that thou incline thine ear unto wisdom, and apply thine heart to understanding.

AMP 2:2   Making your ear attentive to skillful and godly Wisdom and inclining and directing your heart and mind to understanding [applying all your powers to the quest for it];

(Condition): If we accept and believe wisdom's words and store up within us, or mediate upon and memorize wisdom's commands, listening carefully and intently to wisdom and attempting to thoroughly understand, and

Proverbs 2:3

NIV 2:3   and if you call out for insight and cry aloud for understanding...

KJV 2:3   Yea, if thou criest after knowledge, and liftest up thy voice for understanding...

AMP 2:3   Yes, if you cry out for insight and raise your voice for understanding...

(Condition): If we earnestly desire the ability to see into a situation and to obtain complete, thorough, understanding, and

Proverbs 2:4

NIV 2:4   and if you look for it as for silver and search for it as for hidden treasure,

KJV 2:4   If thou seekest her as silver, and searchest for her as for hid treasures;

AMP 2:4   If you seek [Wisdom] as for silver and search for skillful and godly Wisdom as for hidden treasures,

(Condition): If we look for the ability to see into a situation as if it was something very valuable and search for complete, thorough understanding as if it was hidden treasure, (Note: not only is understanding compared to a valuable treasure, but it is also described as "hidden." In other words, we must do some-thing to find this "hidden" understanding. It takes effort on our part to study God's Word to search out the true meaning God has for us.)

Proverbs 2:5

NIV 2:5   then you will understand the fear of the LORD and find the knowledge of God.

KJV 2:5   Then shalt thou understand the fear of the LORD, and find the knowledge of God.

AMP 2:5   Then you will understand the reverent and worshipful fear of the Lord and find the knowledge of [our omniscient] God.

(Result): Then, we will understand the reverence or utmost respect and honor of the Lord and find the knowledge of God or God's knowledge will become our knowledge. We will know what God knows about various subjects. That is exciting!

Proverbs 2:9

NIV 2:9   Then you will understand what is right and just and fair—every good path.

KJV 2:9   Then shalt thou understand righteousness, and judgment, and equity; yea, every good path.

AMP 2:9   Then you will understand righteousness, jus-tice, and fair dealing [in every area and relation]; yes, you will understand every good path.

Verse 9 begins with the word "Then," so we must look at the verses preceding verse 9 to see what must take place before the "result" occurs. If we (1) accept wisdom's words, (2) memorize and meditate to understand, (3) apply our hearts to understanding, (4) seek after insight and understanding, and (5) search for it relentlessly until we find it, then we will understand the reverence of the Lord and find the knowledge of God.

God gives us wisdom and from His Word and through the Holy Spirit come knowledge and understanding. God will cause victory to come to those who live an upright life and will protect those who live a blameless life.

God protects the ways of the just and the faithful. "Then," we will understand what is right, just and fair and what to do in every situation.

Proverbs 3:5

NIV 3:5   Trust in the LORD with all your heart and lean not on your own understanding.

KJV 3:5   Trust in the LORD with all thine heart; and lean not unto thine own understanding.

AMP 3:5   Lean on, trust in, and be confident in the Lord with all your heart and mind and do not rely on your own insight or understanding.

We are to trust in the Lord with all of our heart, which means it is possible to trust in the Lord somewhat, but not entirely. We are not to depend upon our own human understanding. Therefore, we must seek often, until we obtain, the understanding that God reveals to us by studying His Word, praying and listening to God. This "understanding" is much better than our human understanding.

Proverbs 3:13

NIV 3:13 Blessed is the man who finds wisdom, the man who gains understanding...

KJV 3:13 Happy is the man that findeth wisdom, and the man that getteth understanding.

AMP 3:13 Happy (blessed, fortunate, enviable) is the man who finds skillful and godly Wisdom, and the man who gets understanding [drawing it forth from God's Word and life's experiences],

We must "find" wisdom. To "find" something requires an effort to search for it, before you actually find what you are looking for. Once we find wisdom, we will be blessed: To "gain" understanding, we must acquire or get possession of understanding. This too requires effort and action on our part. We must do something before we get this understanding. Once we have understanding, we are blessed. The word "blessed" means "to bring prosperity and happiness upon."

Proverbs 4:5

NIV 4:5 Get wisdom, get understanding; do not forget my words or swerve from them.

KJV 4:5 Get wisdom, get understanding: forget it not; neither decline from the words of my mouth.

AMP 4:5 Get skillful and godly Wisdom, get understanding (discernment, comprehension, and interpretation); do not forget and do not turn back from the words of my mouth.

We are told to "get" wisdom and understanding. Again, this implies something is required of us before we have wisdom and understanding. It takes an effort for a child to listen intently to his or her parents. We are also told not to forget the wise words we learn from our parents and to not do things that we "know" we should not do. The analogy of our Heavenly Father and us can again be used here. It takes effort on our part to study His Word and to pray and listen to Him. We must memorize and meditate on God's Word so that we will not forget it. We have been instructed to stay far away from sin, not to "swerve" from God's Word.

Proverbs 8:1-9

NIV 8:1-9 Does not wisdom call out? Does not understanding raise her voice? On the heights along the way, where the paths meet, she takes her stand; beside the gates leading into the city, at the entrances, she cries aloud: "To you, O men, I call out; I raise my voice to all mankind. You who are simple, gain prudence; you who are foolish, gain understanding. Listen, for I have worthy things to say; I open my lips to speak what is right. My mouth speaks what is true, for my lips detest wickedness. All the words of my mouth are just; none of them is crooked or perverse. To the discerning all of them are right; they are faultless to those who have knowledge."

KJV 8:1-9 Doth not wisdom cry? and understanding

put forth her voice? She standeth in the top of high places, by the way in the places of the paths. She crieth at the gates, at the entry of the city, at the coming in at the doors. Unto you, O men, I call; and my voice is to the sons of man. O ye simple, understand wisdom: and, ye fools, be ye of an understanding heart. Hear; for I will speak of excellent things; and the opening of my lips shall be right things For my mouth shall speak truth; and wickedness is an abomination to my lips. All the words of my mouth are in righteousness; there is nothing froward or perverse in them. They are all plain to him that understandeth, and right to them that find knowledge.

AMP 8:1-9 Does not skillful and godly Wisdom cry out, and understanding raise her voice [in contrast to the loose woman]? On the top of the heights beside the way, where the paths meet, stands Wisdom [skillful and godly]; at the gates at the entrance of the town, at the coming in at the doors, she cries out: To you, O men, I call, and my voice is directed to the sons of men. O you simple and thoughtless ones, understand prudence; you [self-confident] fools, be of an understanding heart. Hear, for I will speak excellent and princely things; and the opening of my lips shall be for right things. For my mouth shall utter truth, and wrongdoing is detestable and loathsome to my lips. All the words of my mouth are righteous (upright and in right standing with God); there is nothing contrary to truth or crooked in them. They are all plain to him who understands [and opens his heart], and right to those who find knowledge [and live by it].

In these nine verses, it is evident that wisdom and understanding are trying to get our attention and stress to us how important it is for all people to listen and understand what they have to say. "Simple" people are those who seem or are unable to use good judgment, discretion or common sense. They are instructed to "gain prudence." "Prudence" is having good judgment or common sense. Notice, people who do not have good judgment or common sense can change and "gain" prudence. Likewise, foolish people (foolish and simple are synonyms, having similar meanings) are instructed to "gain understanding." There is hope for foolish and simple people. However, if they are going to gain or get prudence and understanding, they must humble themselves and choose to do what is required of them and that is to study God's Word, earnestly, with a burning desire to obtain more and more of God's wisdom and understanding. Wisdom and understanding go on to tell us that the things they have for us to learn are "worthy" or very important. What they reveal to us is right, true and just.

Those people who are unable to use sound judgement, discretion or good sense detest or hate wickedness. To those people who have discernment, or the ability to sense what is not evident to other people, all of the words of wisdom and understanding are right. The words of wisdom and understanding are easy to understand to those who have the knowledge that God revealed to them. Therefore, seek God in His Word and communicate with Him and allow God to reveal His wisdom, His understanding and His knowledge to you.

Proverbs 9:10

NIV 9:10   The fear of the LORD is the beginning of wisdom, and knowledge of the Holy One is understanding.

KJV 9:10   The fear of the LORD is the beginning of wisdom: and the knowledge of the holy is understanding.

AMP 9:10   The reverent and worshipful fear of the Lord is the beginning (the chief and choice part) of Wisdom, and the knowledge of the Holy One is insight and understanding.

Obtaining wisdom begins by respecting and reverencing God. Knowledge we gain about God is understanding. The more we study God's Word to gain knowledge, the more understanding God reveals to us. We must just trust God for this understanding and consistently seek to learn more about Him.

Proverbs 16:16

NIV 16:16   How much better to get wisdom than gold, to choose understanding rather than silver!

KJV 16:16   How much better is it to get wisdom than gold! and to get understanding rather to be chosen than silver!

AMP 16:16   How much better it is to get skillful and godly Wisdom than gold! And to get understanding is to be chosen rather than silver.

Having wisdom and understanding will benefit a person in

many areas of life, not just financially. Notice, we must get wisdom and get understanding. This means an effort is required of us. That effort is prayer and studying God's Word.

Proverbs 19:8

NIV 19:8   He who gets wisdom loves his own soul; he who cherishes understanding prospers.

KJV 19:8   He that getteth wisdom loveth his own soul: he that keepeth understanding shall find good.

AMP 19:8   He who gains Wisdom loves his own life; he who keeps understanding shall prosper and find good.

A person who gets or acquires wisdom by doing what is required of him, that is to seek God by studying His Word and praying, wants to become wise in all that he says and does. Those who desire to gain more and more understanding and are willing to put forth the effort to get it by studying and meditating (or pondering) on His Word and praying, will prosper, not only financially, but in all areas of their life.

C. Characteristics of Having Understanding

NIV 11:12   A man who lacks judgment derides his neighbor, but a man of understanding holds his tongue.

KJV 11:12   He that is void of wisdom despiseth his neighbour: but a man of understanding holdeth his peace.

AMP 11:12   He who belittles and despises his neighbor lacks sense, but a man of understanding keeps silent.

A foolish person is someone who lacks good judgment, ridicules or belittles (to "put down") another person, but a person of understanding remains silent.

Proverbs 13:15

NIV 13:15 Good understanding wins favor, but the way of the unfaithful is hard.

KJV 13:15 Good understanding giveth favour: but the way of transgressors is hard.

AMP 13:15 Good understanding wins favor, but the way of the transgressor is hard [like the barren, dry soil or the impassable swamp].

A person with understanding and good sense is respected by others, while the unfaithful sinner will live a hard life.

Proverbs 14:29

NIV 14:29 A patient man has great understanding, but a quick-tempered man displays folly.

KJV 14:29 He that is slow to wrath is of great understanding: but he that is hasty of spirit exalteth folly.

AMP 14:29 He who is slow to anger has great understanding, but he who is hasty of spirit exposes and exalts his folly.

Those who control their anger have great understanding; however, those who have a quick temper display their lack of good sense and prudence.

Proverbs 15:21

NIV 15:21   Folly delights a man who lacks judgment, but a man of understanding keeps a straight course.

KJV 15:21   Folly is joy to him that is destitute of wisdom: but a man of understanding walketh uprightly.

AMP 15:21   Folly is pleasure to him who is without heart and sense, but a man of understanding walks uprightly [making straight his course].

Lacking good sense or prudence brings a "false" joy to those who lack good judgment and wisdom because they do not "know" any different. They think their decisions are good decisions; they do not realize that poor decision after poor decision will bring them heartache, pain and poverty. However, a person of understanding chooses a wise course of action, allowing his decisions to be led and guided by the Holy Spirit.

Proverbs 15:32

NIV 15:32   He who ignores discipline despises himself, but whoever heeds correction gains understanding.

KJV 15:32   He that refuseth instruction despiseth his own soul: but he that heareth reproof getteth understanding.

AMP 15:32   He who refuses and ignores instruction and correction despises himself, but he who heeds reproof gets understanding.

If someone refuses to listen to criticism, he prevents himself from improving. However, if someone does listen to correction, his understanding increases and he becomes wiser.

Proverbs 17:27

NIV 17:27   A man of knowledge uses words with restraint, and a man of understanding is even-tempered.

KJV 17:27   He that hath knowledge spareth his words: and a man of understanding is of an excellent spirit.

AMP 17:27   He who has knowledge spares his words, and a man of understanding has a cool spirit.

Someone who has knowledge thinks before he speaks and chooses his words carefully. A person who has understanding controls his anger.

Proverbs 20:5

NIV 20:5   The purposes of a man's heart are deep waters, but a man of understanding draws them out.

KJV 20:5   Counsel in the heart of man is like deep water; but a man of understanding will draw it out.

AMP 20:5   Counsel in the heart of man is like water in a deep well, but a man of understanding draws it out.

Good advice or good counsel is "revealed" to us by God as we gain understanding and become wise. However, without understanding and wisdom this good advice or good counsel remains "hidden" deep in a person's heart.

Proverbs 24:3

NIV 24:3   By wisdom a house is built, and through understanding it is established;

KJV 24:3   Through wisdom is an house builded; and by understanding it is established:

AMP 24:3   Through skillful and godly Wisdom is a house (a life, a home, a family) built, and by understanding it is established [on a sound and good foundation],

Our bodies are the "temples" of the Holy Spirit. As we obtain wisdom, wisdom becomes the foundation for all that we say and do. We become strengthened or more developed, more mature, as we gain understanding through God revealing it to us.

D. The Rewards of Having Understanding

NIV 2:11   Discretion will protect you, and understanding will guard you.

KJV 2:11   Discretion shall preserve thee, understanding shall keep thee:

AMP 2:11   Discretion shall watch over you, understanding shall keep you.

Discretion or the ability to make responsible decisions will cover or shield you from many potentially harmful things. The understanding that we obtain will protect us from danger.

Proverbs 3:13

NIV 3:13   Blessed is the man who finds wisdom, the man who gains understanding,

KJV 3:13   Happy is the man that findeth wisdom, and the man that getteth understanding.

AMP 3:13   Happy (blessed, fortunate, enviable) is the man who finds skillful and godly Wisdom, and the man who gets understanding [drawing it forth from God's Word and life's experiences],

We must "find" wisdom. To "find" something requires an effort to search for it before you actually find what you are looking for. Once we find wisdom, we will be blessed. To "gain" understanding, we must acquire or get possession of understanding. This too requires effort and action on our part. We must do something before we get this understanding. Once we have understanding, we are blessed. The word "blessed" means "to bring prosperity and happiness upon."

Proverbs 4:7

NIV 4:7   Wisdom is supreme; therefore get wisdom. Though it cost all you have, get understanding.

KJV 4:7   Wisdom is the principal thing; therefore get wisdom: and with all thy getting get understanding.

AMP 4:7   The beginning of Wisdom is: get Wisdom (skillful and godly Wisdom)! [For skillful and godly Wisdom is the principal thing.] And with all you have gotten, get understanding (discernment, comprehension, and interpretation).

Wisdom is the ultimate objective, the most important thing we can have. Therefore, we are instructed to do what we need to do to get wisdom. Regardless of how much effort and time it may take for you to get understanding, you must do what it takes: study His Word, pray and listen. Having wisdom is the most prized possession!

Proverbs 7:4

NIV 7:4   Say to wisdom, "You are my sister," and call understanding your kinsman;

KJV 7:4   Say unto wisdom, Thou art my sister, and call understanding thy kinswoman:

AMP 7:4   Say to skillful and godly Wisdom, You are my sister, and regard understanding or insight as your intimate friend–

Family members are people we see and spend time with every day. We love our family. The same should be true with wisdom and understanding. We should spend time every day studying God's Word and praying, allowing God to reveal His wisdom and His understanding to us. Wisdom and understanding will reveal to you the truth about people. This ability to sense what is not evident to other people is called "discernment."

Proverbs 7:5

NIV 7:5   they will keep you from the adulteress, from the wayward wife with her seductive words.

KJV 7:5   That they may keep thee from the strange woman, from the stranger which flattereth with her words.

AMP 7:5   That they may keep you from the loose wom-
          an, from the adventuress who flatters with
          and makes smooth her words.

By being wise and having understanding, men will know
and realize what consequences they will face if they commit
adultery. The insight and presence of the Holy Spirit will drive
those thoughts and temptations from their minds. When a
married woman seduces a man with her words or body, he will
"sense" in his spirit what she is attempting to do and will know
that what she is suggesting would only bring destruction, un-
happiness and pain. Therefore, wisdom and understanding will
care for and protect you.

Proverbs 8:14

NIV 8:14   Counsel and sound judgment are mine; I
           have understanding and power.

KJV 8:14   Counsel is mine, and sound wisdom: I am
           understanding; I have strength.

AMP 8:14   I have counsel and sound knowledge, I have
           understanding, I have might and power.

If we have wisdom, we will be able to give good advice to
others and we will make wise decisions. Once we have wisdom,
we will also have understanding, insight and power. As we share
our wise ideas and thoughts with others to help them, we will
gain a lot of respect. This "respect" is strengthened as our ideas
become reality and people are helped, and leads to much honor,
promotion and power.

Proverbs 10:23

NIV 10:23 A fool finds pleasure in evil conduct, but a man of understanding delights in wisdom.

KJV 10:23 It is as sport to a fool to do mischief: but a man of understanding hath wisdom.

AMP 10:23 It is as sport to a [self-confident] fool to do wickedness, but to have skillful and godly Wisdom is pleasure and relaxation to a man of understanding.

A foolish person finds gratification in doing wrong and being mean or bad. A man who has understanding enjoys having wisdom and being able to help others with his wisdom.

Proverbs 13:15

NIV 13:15 Good understanding wins favor, but the way of the unfaithful is hard.

KJV 13:15 Good understanding giveth favour: but the way of transgressors is hard.

AMP 13:15 Good understanding wins favor, but the way of the transgressor is hard [like the barren, dry soil or the impassable swamp].

A person with understanding and good sense is respected by others, while the unfaithful sinner will live a hard life.

Proverbs 16:16

NIV 16:16 How much better to get wisdom than gold, to choose understanding rather than silver!

KJV 16:16   How much better is it to get wisdom than gold! And to get understanding rather to be chosen than silver!

AMP 16:16   How much better it is to get skillful and godly Wisdom than gold! And to get understanding is to be chosen rather than silver.

Having wisdom and understanding will benefit a person in many areas of life, not just financially. Notice, we must get wisdom and get understanding. This means an effort is required of us. That effort is prayer and studying God's Word.

Proverbs 16:22

NIV 16:22   Understanding is a fountain of life to those who have it, but folly brings punishment to fools.

KJV 16:22   Understanding is a wellspring of life unto him that hath it: but the instruction of fools is folly.

AMP 16:22   Understanding is a wellspring of life to those who have it, but to give instruction to fools is folly.

To those who have understanding, it will continually bring blessings to their lives. Foolish people, that is, those who lack good judgment or prudence, do not have understanding. Therefore, they can only provide folly, which is a lack of good sense or prudence. Their "foolish" decisions, made repeatedly, will eventually bring ruin to their lives, financially, emotionally and spiritually.

Proverbs 19:8

NIV 19:8   He who gets wisdom loves his own soul; he who cherishes understanding prospers.

KJV 19:8   He that getteth wisdom loveth his own soul: he that keepeth understanding shall find good.

AMP 19:8   He who gains Wisdom loves his own life; he who keeps understanding shall prosper and find good.

A person who gets or acquires wisdom by doing what is required of him, that is, to seek God by studying His Word and praying, wants to become wise in all that he says and does. Those who desire to gain more and more understanding are willing to put forth the effort to get it by studying and meditating (or pondering) on His Word and praying, will prosper, not only financially, but in all areas of their life.

Proverbs 20:5

NIV 20:5   The purposes of a man's heart are deep waters, but a man of understanding draws them out.

KJV 20:5   Counsel in the heart of man is like deep water; but a man of understanding will draw it out.

AMP 20:5   Counsel in the heart of man is like water in a deep well, but a man of understanding draws it out.

Good advice or good counsel are "revealed" to us by God, as we gain understanding and become wise. However, without understanding and wisdom this good advice or good counsel remains "hidden" deep in a person's heart.

Proverbs 28:2

NIV 28:2   When a country is rebellious, it has many rulers, but a man of understanding and knowledge maintains order.

KJV 28:2   For the transgression of a land many are the princes thereof: but by a man of understanding and knowledge the state thereof shall be prolonged.

AMP 28:2   When a land transgresses, it has many rulers, but when the ruler is a man of discernment, understanding, and knowledge, its stability will long continue.

Stability exists when the leaders have wisdom, knowledge and understanding. Wise decisions that are based on knowledge and understanding of situations and circumstances promote stability among those who do not possess these qualities. This is true, whether within a country, a company, a family or any organization.

E. Foolish People "Can" Obtain Understanding If They Do What Is Required

NIV 9:6   Leave your simple ways and you will live; walk in the way of understanding.

KJV 9:6   Forsake the foolish, and live; and go in the way of understanding.

AMP 9:6   Leave off, simple ones [forsake the foolish and simpleminded] and live! And walk in the way of insight and understanding.

If foolish people, that is, those who seem to be unable to use good judgment, discretion or good sense (discretion being the ability to make responsible decisions), seek after wisdom, they will obtain understanding and they will no longer be foolish, but wise in their decision making.

Proverbs 15:21

NIV 15:21 Folly delights a man who lacks judgment, but a man of understanding keeps a straight course.

KJV 15:21 Folly is joy to him that is destitute of wisdom: but a man of understanding walketh uprightly.

AMP 15:21 Folly is pleasure to him who is without heart and sense, but a man of understanding walks uprightly [making straight his course].

Lacking good sense or prudence brings a "false" joy to those who lack good judgment and wisdom because they do not "know" any different. They think their decisions are good decisions; they do not realize that poor decision after poor decision will bring them heartache, pain and poverty. However, a person of understanding chooses a wise course of action, allowing his decisions to be led and guided by the Holy Spirit.

Proverbs 15:32

NIV 15:32 He who ignores discipline despises himself, but whoever heeds correction gains understanding.

KJV 15:32 He that refuseth instruction despiseth his own soul: but he that heareth reproof getteth understanding.

AMP 15:32 He who refuses and ignores instruction and cor-

rection despises himself, but he who
heeds reproof gets understanding.

If someone refuses to listen to criticism, he prevents himself from improving. However, if someone does listen to correction, his understanding increases and he becomes wiser.

Proverbs 16:22

NIV 16:22   Understanding is a fountain of life to those who have it, but folly brings punishment to fools.

KJV 16:22   Understanding is a wellspring of life unto him that hath it: but the instruction of fools is folly.

AMP 16:22 Understanding is a wellspring of life to those who have it, but to give instruction to fools is folly.

To those who have understanding, it will continually bring blessings to their lives. Foolish people, that is, those who lack good judgment or prudence, do not have understanding. Therefore, they can only provide folly, which is a lack of good sense or prudence. Their "foolish" decisions made repeatedly will eventually bring ruin to their lives, financially, emotionally and spiritually.

Proverbs 18:2

NIV 18:2   A fool finds no pleasure in understanding but delights in airing his own opinions.

KJV 18:2   A fool hath no delight in understanding, but that his heart my discover itself.

AMP 18:2   A [self-confident] fool has no delight in

understanding but only in revealing his personal opinions and himself.

A fool, that is a person who lacks good judgment or prudence, does not have understanding and is not interested in understanding. He enjoys talking a lot to tell others what his opinions are. He would rather talk than listen and learn. He thinks he already "knows everything."

Proverbs 21:16

NIV 21:16 A man who strays from the path of understanding comes to rest in the company of the dead.

KJV 21:16 The man that wandereth out of the way of understanding shall remain in the congregation of the dead.

AMP 21:16 A man who wanders out of the way of understanding shall abide in the congregation of the spirits (of the dead).

If a person has been seeking more of the knowledge of God by studying His Word and praying and then he stops doing the things required of him to gain understanding, he will find himself back in the same situations and circumstances as those who never attempted to obtain the knowledge of God or to gain understanding. He will find himself spending his time with those people who are spiritually dead.

III

WISDOM

A. The Beginning of Wisdom

1. God Created Wisdom

NIV 8:22 The LORD brought me forth as the first of his works, before his deeds of old;

KJV 8:22 The LORD possessed me in the beginning of his way, before his works of old.

AMP 8:22 The LORD formed and brought me [Wisdom] forth at the beginning of His way, before His acts of old.

God created wisdom first, before He created anything else.

Proverbs 8:23

NIV 8:23 I was appointed from eternity, from the beginning, before the world began.

KJV 8:23 I was set up from everlasting, from the beginning, or ever the earth was.

AMP 8:23 [Wisdom] was inaugurated and ordained from everlasting, from the beginning, before ever the earth existed.

Wisdom was fixed or set officially from the beginning of everything, way before the creation of the earth.

Proverbs 8:24-26

NIV 8:24-26   When there were no oceans, I was given birth, when there were no springs abounding with water; before the mountains were settled in place, before the hills, I was given birth, before he made the earth or its fields or any of the dust of the world.

KJV 8:24-26   When there were no depths, I was brought forth; when there were no fountains abounding with water. Before the mountains were settled, before the hills was I brought forth: While as yet he had not made the earth, nor the fields, nor the highest part of the dust of the world.

AMP 8:24-26   When there were no deeps, I was brought forth, when there were no fountains laden with water. Before the mountains were settled, before the hills, I was brought forth, While as yet He had not made the land or the fields or the first of the dust of the earth.

(Verse 24): Wisdom was created before God made the earth, its fields or any of the dirt.

(Verse 25): Wisdom was created before the oceans and the springs. Wisdom was created before the mountains and the hills.

(Verse 26): Wisdom was created before God made the earth, its fields or any of the dirt.

2. God Used Wisdom

NIV 3:19 By wisdom the LORD laid the earth's foundations, by understanding he set the heavens in place;

KJV 3:19 The LORD by wisdom hath founded the earth; by understanding hath he established the heavens.

AMP 3:19 The LORD by skillful and godly Wisdom has founded the earth; by understanding He has established the heavens.

God used wisdom to create the earth and He used understanding to establish or create the heavens.

Proverbs 8:27

NIV 8:27 I was there when he set the heavens in place, when he marked out the horizon on the face of the deep,

KJV 8:27 When he prepared the heavens, I was there: when he set a compass upon the face of the depth:

AMP 8:27 When He prepared the heavens, I [Wisdom] was there; when He drew a circle upon the face of the deep and stretched out the firmament over it,

Wisdom was there when God created the heavens and when He made all the intricate details of the earth.

Proverbs 8:28

NIV 8:28   when he established the clouds above and fixed securely the fountains of the deep,

KJV 8:28   When he established the clouds above: when he strengthened the fountains of the deep:

AMP 8:28   When He made firm the skies above, when He established the fountains of the deep,

Wisdom was there when God created the clouds and the deep fountains of water that originally provided water for everything on the earth.

Proverbs 8:29

NIV 8:29   When he gave the sea its boundary so the waters would not overstep his command, and when he marked out the foundations of the earth.

KJV 8:29   When he gave to the sea his decree, that the waters should not pass his commandment: when he appointed the foundations of the earth:

AMP 8:29   When He gave to the sea its limit and His decree that the waters should not transgress [across the boundaries set by] His command, when He appointed the foundations of the earth –

Wisdom was there when God created land that was above the water, limiting where the water could go and when He placed the foundations of the earth.

3. Wisdom Brought God Great Joy

NIV 8:30   Then I was the craftsman at his side. I was filled with delight day after day, rejoicing always in his presence,

KJV 8:30   Then I was by him, as one brought up with him: and I was daily his delight, rejoicing always before him;

AMP 8:30   Then I [Wisdom] was beside Him as a master and director of the work; and I was daily His delight, rejoicing before Him always,

Then, wisdom was God's "helper" and wisdom gave God great pleasure, extreme satisfaction and a high degree of gratification every day. Wisdom always brought joy or great delight to God.

Proverbs 8:31

NIV 8:31   rejoicing in his whole world and delighting in mankind.

KJV 8:31   Rejoicing in the habitable part of his earth; and my delights were with the sons of men.

AMP 8:31   Rejoicing in His inhabited earth and delighting in the sons of men.

Wisdom was very pleased with the part of the earth where people were to live and was extremely satisfied with the creation of human beings.

4. Respect and Honor the Lord Is Where We Begin

NIV 1:7   The fear of the Lord is the beginning of knowledge, but fools despise wisdom and discipline

KJV 1:7   The fear of the LORD is the beginning of knowledge: but fools despise wisdom and instruction.

AMP 1:7   The reverent and worshipful fear of the Lord is the beginning and the principal and choice part of knowledge [its starting point and its essence]; but fools despise skillful and godly Wisdom, instruction, and discipline.

The respect and honor of the Lord is where we begin in our pursuit of obtaining knowledge. Fools despise or hate wisdom and instruction.

Proverbs 9:10

NIV 9:10   The fear of the LORD is the beginning of wisdom, and knowledge of the Holy One is understanding.

KJV 9:10   The fear of the LORD is the beginning of wisdom: and the knowledge of the holy is understanding.

AMP 9:10   The reverent and worshipful fear of the Lord is the beginning (the chief and choice part) of Wisdom, and the knowledge of the Holy One is insight and understanding.

Before we can obtain wisdom, we must fear or have a "reverential awe" of God. This "reverential awe" can be described as honor, respect and profound adoring. As we obtain knowledge of God by studying His Word, understanding is revealed to us.

B. The Purpose of Having Wisdom

NIV 1:2   for attaining wisdom and discipline; for understanding words of insight;

KJV 1:2   To know wisdom and instruction; to perceive the words of understanding;

AMP 1:2   That people may know skillful and godly Wisdom and instruction, discern and comprehend the words of understanding and insight,

The proverbs were written for a purpose, to teach people wisdom (the ability to discern and choose a wise course of action) and discipline (to train by instruction and control) and for understanding words of insight (or discernment, the ability to see into a situation).

1. So We Can Know What Is "Right"

NIV 8:6   Listen, for I have worthy things to say; I open my lips to speak what is right.

KJV 8:6   Hear; for I will speak of excellent things; and the opening of my lips shall be right things.

AMP 8:6   Hear, for I will speak excellent and princely things; and the opening of my lips shall be for right things.

We are to listen to wisdom because wisdom has very important things to teach us. The purpose of wisdom when it speaks to us is to speak what is "right." If we want to always know what is "right," we must listen to what wisdom is telling us.

2. Wisdom Is Used By Many People

NIV 8:15   By me kings reign and rulers make laws that are just;

KJV 8:15   By me kings reign, and princes decree justice.

AMP 8:15   By me kings reign and rulers decree justice.

Kings use wisdom to reign, rulers use wisdom to create laws that are just or fair.

Proverbs 8:16

NIV 8:16   by me princes govern, and all nobles who rule on earth.

KJV 8:16   By me princes rule, and nobles, even all the judges of the earth.

AMP 8:16   By me princes rule, and nobles, even all the judges and governors of the earth.

Rulers use wisdom to govern or lead people. Judges and other people in authority also use wisdom.

C. Who Can Have Wisdom?

1. Wisdom Is Available to Everyone

NIV 1:20-21   Wisdom calls aloud in the street, she raises her voice in the public squares; at the head of the noisy streets she cries out, in the gateways of the city she makes her speech:

KJV 1:20-21   Wisdom crieth without; she uttereth her voice in the streets: She crieth in the chief place of concourse, in the openings of the gates: in the city she uttereth her words, saying,

AMP 1:20-21   Wisdom cries aloud in the street, she raises her voice in the markets; She cries at the head of the noisy intersections [in the chief gathering place]; at the entrance of the city gates she speaks:

Proverbs 8:1

NIV 8:1   Does not wisdom call out? Does not understanding raise her voice?

KJV 8:1   Doth not wisdom cry? and understanding put forth her voice?

AMP 8:1   Does not skillful and godly Wisdom cry out, and understanding raise her voice [in contrast to the loose woman]?

Wisdom and understanding are available to everyone. However, many people choose to ignore them.

Proverbs 8:4

NIV 8:4   To you, O men, I call out; I raise my voice to all mankind.

KJV 8:4   Unto you, O men, I call; and my voice is to the sons of man.

AMP 8:4   To you, O men, I call, and my voice is directed to the sons of men.

Wisdom is available to everyone! God wants to give everyone His wisdom. However, the decision to get wisdom is entirely up to each of us.

Proverbs 9:1-2

NIV 9:1-2   Wisdom has built her house; she has hewn out its seven pillars. She has prepared her meat and mixed her wine; she has also set her table. She has sent out her maids, and she calls from the highest point of the city.

KJV 9:1-2   Wisdom hath builded her house, she hath hewn out her seven pillars: She hath killed her beasts; she hath mingled her wine; she hath also furnished her table. She hath sent forth her maidens: she crieth upon the highest places of the city,

AMP 9:1-2   Wisdom has built her house; she has hewn out and set up her seven [perfect number of] pillars. She has killed her beasts, she has mixed her [spiritual] wine; she has also set her table.

She has sent out her maids to cry from the
highest places of the town:

Wisdom can provide us everything we need! Wisdom is
available to everyone. Wisdom offers those people who are unable or unwilling to use good judgment, discretion or good sense
to listen to and accept wisdom's teachings. If those "simple"
people would turn to wisdom and seek to find wisdom in God's
Word, God would give wisdom to them. God prefers everyone
to have wisdom. However, He leaves the choice up to us.

D. How To Get Wisdom

1. What Is the Beginning of Wisdom?

NIV 9:10   The fear of the LORD is the beginning of
wisdom, and knowledge of the Holy One is
understanding.

KJV 9:10   The fear of the LORD is the beginning of
wisdom: and the knowledge of the holy is
understanding.

AMP 9:10   The reverent and worshipful fear of the Lord
is the beginning (the chief and choice part)
of Wisdom, and the knowledge of the Holy
One is insight and understanding.

Before we can obtain wisdom, we must fear or have a "reverential awe" of God. This "reverential awe" can be described as
honor, respect and profound adoring. As we obtain knowledge
of God by studying His Word, understanding is revealed to us.

2. We Must Humble Ourselves Before God

NIV 11:2   When pride comes, then comes disgrace, but with humility comes wisdom.

KJV 11:2   When pride cometh, then cometh shame: but with the lowly is wisdom.

AMP 11:2   When swelling and pride come, then emptiness and shame come also, but with the humble (those who are lowly, who have been pruned or chiseled by trial, and renounce self) are skillful and godly Wisdom and soundness.

When a person becomes "arrogant," that is when someone exaggerates one's own worth or importance in an overbearing manner, then that person will experience a loss of honor and esteem, will acquire a bad reputation and complete humiliation. However, a person who is humble will have wisdom. We must "humble" ourselves before God in order for us to "reverence" Him and reverencing God is the requirement for obtaining wisdom.

3. How Important Is It To Get Wisdom?

NIV 4:7   Wisdom is supreme; therefore get wisdom. Though it cost all you have, get understanding.

KJV 4:7   Wisdom is the principal thing; therefore get wisdom: and with all thy getting get understanding.

AMP 4:7   The beginning of Wisdom is: get Wisdom (skillful and godly Wisdom)! [For skillful and godly Wisdom is the principal thing.] And with all you have gotten, get understanding (discernment, comprehension, and interpretation).

Wisdom is the most important thing to have. Therefore, above all else, we should do what is required to get wisdom. As we are "getting" or obtaining wisdom, we are to get understanding.

Proverbs 4:8

NIV 4:8   Esteem her, and she will exalt you; embrace her, and she will honor you.

KJV 4:8   Exalt her, and she shall promote thee: she shall bring thee to honour, when thou dost embrace her.

AMP 4:8   Prize Wisdom highly and exalt her, and she will exalt and promote you; she will bring you to honor when you embrace her.

If we value wisdom enough to strive to get it, that is, if we spend time studying and meditating upon God's Word, then we will have wisdom.

4. Where Do We Get Wisdom?

NIV 2:6   For the LORD gives wisdom, and from his mouth come knowledge and understanding.

KJV 2:6   For the LORD giveth wisdom: out of his mouth cometh knowledge and understanding.

AMP 2:6   For the Lord gives skillful and godly Wisdom; from His mouth come knowledge and understanding.

The Lord is where we can get wisdom. From His "mouth" come knowledge and understanding. God "speaks" to us through His Word and through the Holy Spirit.

Proverbs 3:13

NIV 3:13   Blessed is the man who finds wisdom, the man who gains understanding.

KJV 3:13   Happy is the man that findeth wisdom, and the man that getteth understanding.

AMP 3:13   Happy (blessed, fortunate, enviable) is the man who finds skillful and godly Wisdom, and the man who gets understanding [drawing it forth from God's Word and life's experiences],

Notice, wisdom is something that requires action from us; we must "find" it. In order to "find" it, we must "search" for it. How do we search for wisdom? (1) We ask God to give us wisdom, (2) We do our part and read, study and meditate upon God's Word, (3) We act upon His Word and do what God tells us to do; we obey God. The man who finds wisdom will be blessed and happy. Notice, the man who gets or obtains understanding is also blessed and happy. We get understanding the same way. God will reveal understanding of His Word to us through His Holy Spirit.

5. What We Must Do To Get Wisdom

NIV 19:8   He who gets wisdom loves his own soul; he who cherishes understanding prospers.

KJV 19:8   He that getteth wisdom loveth his own soul: he that keepeth understanding shall find good.

AMP 19:8   He who gains Wisdom loves his own life; he who keeps understanding shall prosper and find good.

A person who gets or acquires wisdom by doing what is required of him, that is to seek God by studying His Word and praying, wants to become wise in all that he says and does. Those who desire to gain more and more understanding and are willing to put forth the effort to gain it by studying, meditating or pondering on His Word and praying, will prosper, not only financially, but in all areas of their life.

6. Wisdom Is Easily Understood By Those Who Have Obtained Knowledge and Understanding

NIV 8:9   To the discerning all of them are right; they are faultless to those who have knowledge.

KJV 8:9   They are all plain to him that understandeth, and right to them that find knowledge.

AMP 8:9   They are all plain to him who understands [and opens his heart], and right to those who find knowledge [and live by it].

To those people who have "understanding," all the words of wisdom are easily understood. To those who have "found" knowledge, all the words of wisdom are right. Notice, we must "seek after" knowledge to "find" it. We do this by studying God's Word. God will reveal His knowledge to us.

7. We Are to Concentrate on Understanding Wisdom's Teachings

NIV 4:20   My son, pay attention to what I say; listen closely to my words.

KJV 4:20   My son, attend to my words; incline thine ear unto my sayings.

AMP 4:20   My son, attend to my words; consent and submit to my sayings.

We are to listen intently to what wisdom (God's Word) is teaching us. We should concentrate on listening and understanding wisdom's words, in order for us to know it well enough to be able to speak the words to release God's power in our lives and in other people's lives.

8. We Are to Love and Cherish Wisdom and Understanding

NIV 7:4   Say to wisdom, "You are my sister," and call understanding your kinsman;

KJV 7:4   Say unto wisdom, Thou art my sister; and call understanding thy kinswoman:

AMP 7:4   Say to skillful and godly Wisdom, You are my sister, and regard understanding or insight as your intimate friend–

We love and cherish our family members. In the same way, we are to love and cherish wisdom and understanding.

9. Wisdom Loves Us If We Love Wisdom

NIV 8:17   I love those who love me, and those who seek me find me.

KJV 8:17   I love them that love me; and those that seek me early shall find me.

AMP 8:17   I love those who love me, and those who seek me early and diligently shall find me.

Wisdom "loves" us if we love wisdom. When we love someone, we find a way to spend time with them and we enjoy being around them. The same is true with wisdom. If we love wisdom, we will spend time in God's Word so that God can continue to give us wisdom. For those of us who "look for" wisdom (in God's Word), we will definitely find it!

10. We Must Humble Ourselves and Listen to Advice of Wise People

NIV 5:1   My son, pay attention to my wisdom, listen well to my words of insight.

KJV 5:1   My son, attend unto my wisdom, and bow thine ear to my understanding:

AMP 5:1   My son, be attentive to my Wisdom [godly Wisdom learned by actual and costly experience], and incline your ear to my understanding [of what is becoming and prudent for you].

We are to listen carefully to the words and advice of a wise person and to learn by listening to their words of insight and understanding. We must humble ourselves and be "teachable."

Proverbs 19:20

NIV 19:20 Listen to advice and accept instruction, and

in the end you will be wise.

KJV 19:20   Hear counsel, and receive instruction, that thou mayest be wise in thy latter end.

AMP 19:20   Hear counsel, receive instruction, and accept correction, that you may be wise in the time to come.

In order to become wise, a person must be willing to listen to advice given by others and be willing to accept instruction, in other words, be teachable.

11. Wise People Listen to Other Wise People to Become Even Wiser

NIV 18:15   The heart of the discerning acquires knowledge; the ears of the wise seek it out.

KJV 18:15   The heart of the prudent getteth knowledge; and the ear of the wise seeketh knowledge.

AMP 18:15   The mind of the prudent is ever getting knowledge, and the ear of the wise is ever seeking (inquiring for and craving) knowledge.

The person who has good judgment and common sense really wants to acquire more knowledge. The wise person listens to others to see if he can acquire more knowledge from what they say.

12. Blessed Are Those People Who Do as Wisdom Instructs

NIV 8:34   Blessed is the man who listens to me, watching

daily at my doors, waiting at my doorway.

KJV 8:34   Blessed is the man that heareth me, watching daily at my gates, waiting at the posts of my doors.

AMP 8:34   Blessed (happy, fortunate, to be envied) is the man who listens to me, watching daily at my gates, waiting at the posts of my doors.

Blessed are those who listen to wisdom, searching daily for more wisdom and to use the wisdom they have, always looking to become wiser.

E. Characteristics of Having Wisdom

1. Righteous, Upright, Good and Obedient

NIV 8:8   All the words of my mouth are just; none of them is crooked or perverse.

KJV 8:8   All the words of my mouth are in rightousness; there is nothing froward or perverse in them.

AMP 8:8   All the words of my mouth are righteous (upright and in right standing with God); there is nothing contrary to truth or crooked in them.

All of wisdom's words are "just," which means righteous, upright or good. There is nothing "froward," which means being habitually disobedient and opposing or adverse, in wisdom's words. Neither is there anything "perverse," which is being turned away from what is right or good, in wisdom's words.

2. Wins Souls

NIV 11:30 The fruit of the righteous is a tree of life, and he who wins souls is wise.

KJV 11:30 The fruit of the righteous is a tree of life; and he that winneth souls is wise.

AMP 11:30 The fruit of the [uncompromisingly] righteous is a tree of life, and he who is wise captures human lives [for God, as a fisher of men–he gathers and receives them for eternity].

The "righteous" are those people who are free from guilt or sin, acting in accord with divine law, the Word of God. If you have accepted Jesus into your heart and have made Him the Lord of your life, you are the "righteous" in Christ Jesus. The word "life" here means spiritual existence transcending physical death. The phrase "tree of life" represents many people's lives that a "righteous" person has led to accept Jesus into their hearts. The word "fruit" here means the result of an action. Therefore, we can say it this way: The results of a born-again Christian should be leading many other people to accept Jesus also. The rest of the verse says the person that "wins souls" is wise. "Wins souls" means to share Jesus with others and lead them to accept Jesus Christ into their heart and make Him the Lord of their life.

3. Lives a Godly Lifestyle

NIV 15:24 The path of life leads upward for the wise to keep him from going down to the grave.

KJV 15:24 The way of life is above to the wise, that he may depart from hell beneath.

AMP 15:24   The path of the wise leads upward to life, that he may avoid [the gloom] in the depths of Sheol (Hades, the place of the dead).

A wise person makes wise decisions. He accepts Jesus Christ as his Savior. He chooses a godly lifestyle daily so that he may be pleasing to God and not go to hell!

4. Stores Up Knowledge

NIV 10:14   Wise men store up knowledge, but the mouth of a fool invites ruin.

KJV 10:14   Wise men lay up knowledge: but the mouth of the foolish is near destruction.

AMP 10:14   Wise men store up knowledge [in mind and heart], but the mouth of the foolish is a present destruction.

Wise people, that is, people who have a capacity for sound judgment, keen discernment and deep understanding, store up knowledge.

Proverbs 18:15

NIV 18:15   The heart of the discerning acquires knowledge; the ears of the wise seek it out.

KJV 18:15   The heart of the prudent getteth knowledge; and the ear of the wise seeketh knowledge.

AMP 18:15   The mind of the prudent is ever getting knowledge, and the ear of the wise is ever seeking (inquiring for and craving) knowledge.

The person who has good judgment and common sense really wants to acquire more knowledge. The wise person listens to others to see if he can acquire more knowledge from what they say.

5. Speaks Uplifting Words to Others

NIV 12:18   Reckless words pierce like a sword, but the tongue of the wise brings healing.

KJV 12:18   There is that speaketh like the piercings of a sword: but the tongue of the wise is health.

AMP 12:18   There are those who speak rashly, like the piercing of a sword, but the tongue of the wise brings healing.

Some people say words to others that hurt them severely, but the words of wise people cause those who hear them to be sound and flourish in body, mind and spirit.

6. Speaks Kind Words

NIV 16:21   The wise in heart are called discerning, and pleasant words promote instruction.

KJV 16:21   The wise in heart shall be called prudent: and the sweetness of the lips increaseth learning.

AMP 16:21   The wise in heart are called prudent, understanding and knowing, and winsome speech increases learning [in both speaker and listener].

The wise person shall be looked upon by others as having good judgment and common sense. Kind words he speaks will be well received by those who hear them. The opposite is also true. If a person speaks harsh words, they will not be well received by those who hear them.

Proverbs 31:26

NIV 31:26   She speaks with wisdom, and faithful instruction is on her tongue.

KJV 31:26   She openeth her mouth with wisdom; and in her tongue is the law of kindness.

AMP 31:26   She opens her mouth in skillful and godly Wisdom, and on her tongue is the law of kindness [giving counsel and instruction].

A wife of noble character speaks words of wisdom. The words that she speaks demonstrate the "law" of kindness, which means the way she speaks words of kindness is commonly regarded as a guide or an example for others to follow. A wife who has "noble" character is one who has very high or excellent qualities.

7. Distributes Knowledge with His Words

NIV 15:7   The lips of the wise spread knowledge; not so the hearts of fools.

KJV 15:7   The lips of the wise disperse knowledge: but the heart of the foolish doeth not so.

AMP 15:7   The lips of the wise disperse knowledge [sifting it as chaff from the grain]; not so the minds and hearts of the self-confident and foolish.

The words spoken by the wise person distribute knowledge to those who listen to them.

8. Is Greatly Valued By Someone Who Received and Obeyed Correction

NIV 25:12   Like an earring of gold or an ornament of fine gold is a wise man's rebuke to a listening ear.

KJV 25:12   As an earring of gold, and an ornament of fine gold, so is a wise reprover upon an obedient ear.

AMP 25:12   Like an earring or nose ring of gold or an ornament of fine gold is a wise reprover to an ear that listens and obeys.

A wise person who reproves, which is to scold or correct, usually gently or with kind intent, is greatly valued by the person who receives the correction, just as a person would highly value jewelry made from the finest gold.

9. Willing to Listen to Advice

NIV 1:5-6   let the wise listen and add to their learning, and let the discerning get guidance–for understanding proverbs and parables, the sayings and riddles of the wise.

KJV 1:5-6   a wise man will hear, and will increase learning; and a man of understanding shall attain unto wise counsels: To understand a proverb, and the interpretation; the words of the wise, and their dark sayings.

AMP 1:5-6 The wise also will hear and increase learning, and the person of understanding will acquire skill and attain to sound counsel [so that he may be able to steer his course rightly]—That people may understand a proverb and a figure of speech or an enigma with its interpretation, and the words of the wise and their dark sayings or riddles

A wise person will be willing to listen and eager to add to what he already knows. A discerning person, or a person who has the ability to sense what is not evident to other people, will receive guidance for understanding proverbs and parables, and what is truly meant by the wise person's sayings.

Proverbs 12:15

NIV 12:15 The way of a fool seems right to him, but a wise man listens to advice.

KJV 12:15 The way of a fool is right in his own eyes: but he that hearkeneth unto counsel is wise.

AMP 12:15 The way of a fool is right in his own eyes, but he who listens to counsel is wise.

However, the person who will listen to advice is wise.

Proverbs 13:10

NIV 13:10 Pride only breeds quarrels, but wisdom is found in those who take advice.

KJV 13:10 Only by pride cometh contention: but with the well advised is wisdom.

AMP 13:10 By pride and insolence comes only contention, but with the well-advised is skillful and godly Wisdom.

Contention, that is strife or competition that shows itself in quarrelling, disputing or controversy, is caused by pride, which is having or displaying excessive self-esteem. However, those who have listened to advice have God-given wisdom that will benefit them. Again, we are to humble ourselves and not think too highly of ourselves.

Proverbs 21:11

NIV 21:11 When a mocker is punished, the simple gain wisdom; when a wise man is instructed, he gets knowledge.

KJV 21:11 When the scorner is punished, the simple is made wise: and when the wise is instructed, he receiveth knowledge.

AMP 21:11 When the scoffer is punished, the fool gets a lesson in being wise; but men of [godly] Wisdom and good sense learn by being instructed.

When the scorner, a person who openly shows dislike, disrespect and contempt, is punished, the simple, that is the person who is unable to use sound judgment, discretion or good sense is made wise or learns from it. When the wise person is instructed, he is willing to listen and by doing so, he receives knowledge.

10. Gives Wise Advice and Speaks Words of Wisdom

NIV 10:13 Wisdom is found on the lips of the discerning, but a rod is for the back of him who lacks judgment.

KJV 10:13 In the lips of him that hath understanding wisdom is found: but a rod is for the back of him that is void of understanding.

AMP 10:13 On the lips of him who has discernment skillful and godly Wisdom is found, but discipline and the rod are for the back of him who is without sense and understanding.

People who have "understanding" will speak wise words. Those people who do not have understanding will suffer the consequences of bad decisions, which will negatively affect all areas of their life.

Proverbs 10:31

NIV 10:31 The mouth of the righteous brings forth wisdom, but a perverse tongue will be cut out.

KJV 10:31 The mouth of the just bringeth forth wisdom: but the froward tongue shall be cut out.

AMP 10:31 The mouths of the righteous (those harmonious with God) bring forth skillful and godly Wisdom, but the perverse tongue shall be cut down [like a barren and rotten tree].

The righteous person, that is, someone who is in "right

standing with God," gives wise advice and speaks words of wisdom. The tongue of a person who is habitually speaking words of disobedience and opposition, that is turned away from what is right or good, shall be "cut out." If a tongue is "cut out," that person would not be able to speak any longer. If he cannot speak, then others will not listen. In other words, people will get to the point of not wanting to hear negative words all the time and "tune out" that person's words and avoid being around them.

Proverbs 13:14

NIV 13:14 The teaching of the wise is a fountain of life, turning a man from the snares of death.

KJV 13:14 The law of the wise is a fountain of life, to depart from the snares of death.

AMP 13:14 The teaching of the wise is a fountain of life, that one may avoid the snares of death.

The word "law" is a principle or rule of behavior commonly accepted as a valid guide. Therefore, the principles or rules of behavior of the wise person are a "fountain of life." The word "fountain" here means "source" and the word "life" here means a principle that is considered to underlie the "quality of life." Therefore, the principles or rules of behavior of the wise person are the source that determines the quality of life of a person. In other words, if you make wise decisions daily, they will cause you to have a high quality of life in all areas.

Proverbs 13:14

NIV 13:14 The teaching of the wise is a fountain of life, turning a man from the snares of death.

KJV 13:14   The law of the wise is a fountain of life, to depart from the snares of death.

AMP 13:14   The teaching of the wise is a fountain of life, that one may avoid the snares of death.

The second part of this verse addresses departing from the "snares" of "death." The word "snares" means something by which one is entangled, involved in difficulties, or impeded, something deceptively attractive, or a trap. The word "death" here is the contradiction or opposite of the word "life" in the first part of the verse, representing the "quality of life" a person has. Therefore, in summary, if we follow the principles, ways of behavior and the decision making of a wise person, we will have a high quality of life and will avoid the deceptive "lures" of life that would cause our quality of life to be poor and miserable.

Proverbs 15:2

NIV 15:2   The tongue of the wise commends knowledge, but the mouth of the fool gushes folly.

KJV 15:2   The tongue of the wise useth knowledge aright: but the mouth of fools poureth out foolishness.

AMP 15:2   The tongue of the wise utters knowledge rightly, but the mouth of the [self-confident] fool pours out folly.

The wise person speaks words from his knowledge correctly, which means to help and give good advice to other people; however, the words of fools, people who lack good judgment, prudence and understanding, are foolishness, or their ideas are absurd, ridiculous and based on poor judgment.

Proverbs 18:4

NIV 18:4   The words of a man's mouth are deep waters, but the fountain of wisdom is a bubbling brook.

KJV 18:4   The words of a man's mouth are as deep waters, and the wellspring of wisdom as a flowing brook.

AMP 18:4   The words of a [discreet and wise] man's mouth are like deep waters [plenteous and difficult to fathom], and the fountain of skillful and godly Wisdom is like a gushing stream [sparkling, fresh, pure, and life-giving].

The words of a person are as deep waters, or plentiful. He speaks lots of words. However, when a person speaks "words of wisdom," it is a wellspring, giving endless hope and wise advice. It is like a flowing brook, continuously giving refreshing ideas and words of wisdom.

11. Capable of Giving Good Advice and Making Sound Judgment or Decisions

NIV 8:14   Counsel and sound judgment are mine; I have understanding and power.

KJV 8:14   Counsel is mine, and sound wisdom: I am understanding; I have strength.

AMP 8:14   I have counsel and sound knowledge, I have understanding, I have might and power.

When we have wisdom we will be able to give good advice and make sound judgments or decisions. When we have wisdom, we have understanding and power.

12. Has Discernment Whether Advice Is Good or Bad

NIV 9:9   Instruct a wise man and he will be wiser still; teach a righteous man and he will add to his learning.

KJV 9:9   Give instruction to a wise man, and he will be yet wiser: teach a just man, and he will increase in learning.

AMP 9:9   Give instruction to a wise man and he will be yet wiser; teach a righteous man (one upright and in right standing with God) and he will increase in learning.

A wise person has discernment which allows him to know if instruction being given to him is good advice or bad advice. If it is good advice, he will accept it and add it to the understanding, knowledge and wisdom he already has and become even wiser. Teach a just man, that is, a person acting or being in conformity with what is morally upright or good, and he will add to the knowledge and understanding he has.

13. Thinks Before He Speaks and Chooses His Words Wisely

NIV 10:19 When words are many, sin is not absent, but he who holds his tongue is wise.

KJV 10:19 In the multitude of words there wanteth not

sin: but he that refraineth his lips is wise.

AMP 10:19 In a multitude of words transgression is not lacking, but he who restrains his lips is prudent.

A person who talks "too much" usually has sin in their life, but a person who thinks before he speaks and chooses his words carefully is wise.

Proverbs 16:14

NIV 16:14 A king's wrath is a messenger of death, but a wise man will appease it.

KJV 16:14 The wrath of a king is as messengers of death: but a wise man will pacify it.

AMP 16:14 The wrath of a king is as messengers of death, but a wise man will pacify it.

The strong, vengeful anger of a king could lead to one's death in the days when the Bible was written; however, a wise man knows what to do and say to appease the king's anger, thus avoiding harm to himself. A "king" today can be someone who is in a position of authority over another.

Proverbs 16:23

NIV 16:23 A wise man's heart guides his mouth, and his lips promote instruction.

KJV 16:23 The heart of the wise teacheth his mouth, and addeth learning to his lips.

AMP 16:23 The mind of the wise instructs his mouth, and

adds learning and persuasiveness to his lips.

The wise person listens to his heart or spirit before he speaks; therefore, the words he speaks teach those who hear them. The things we take into our minds by what we see with our eyes and hear with our ears will go into our hearts and become what we believe. When we speak, the words we say, how we say them and in what tone of voice we speak them will affect those who hear them. The wise person has deposited knowledge, understanding and wisdom into his heart by studying God's Word and listening to wise advice with his mind (through his eyes and ears). When he speaks, wise words will come out of his heart into his mind and be spoken. He will learn to draw upon this inner wisdom that has developed prior to speaking.

Proverbs 29:11

NIV 29:11   A fool gives full vent to his anger, but a wise man keeps himself under control.

KJV 29:11   A fool uttereth all his mind: but a wise man keepeth it in till afterwards.

AMP 29:11   A [self-confident] fool utters all his anger, but a wise man holds it back and stills it.

A wise person thinks about what he is going to say before he says it. A wise person "keeps his thoughts in his mind" until after he thinks about what words he is going to speak.

14. Listens to Constructive Criticism

NIV 15:31   He who listens to a life-giving rebuke will be at home among the wise.

KJV 15:31   The ear that heareth the reproof of life abideth among the wise.

AMP 15:31   The ear that listens to the reproof [that leads to or gives] life will remain among the wise.

The person who listens to constructive criticism for a fault, usually made gently or with a kind intent, is considered wise.

15. Remains Quiet When He Could Respond in Defense or Retaliation

NIV 17:28   Even a fool is thought wise if he keeps silent, and discerning if he holds his tongue.

KJV 17:28   Even a fool, when he holdeth his peace, is counted wise: and he that shutteth his lips is esteemed a man of understanding.

AMP 17:28   Even a fool when he holds his peace is considered wise; when he closes his lips he is esteemed a man of understanding.

Even a person who lacks good judgment, prudence or understanding is considered wise when he remains quiet when it would be easy to react with a response in defense or retaliation. The person who remains quiet at such times is highly regarded by others as a person of understanding.

16. Controls His Anger

NIV 19:11   A man's wisdom gives him patience; it is to his glory to overlook an offense

KJV 19:11   The discretion of a man deferreth his anger;

and it is his glory to pass over a transgression.

AMP 19:11 Good sense makes a man restrain his anger,
and it is his glory to overlook a transgression
or an offense.

The ability of a wise person to make responsible decisions
causes him to delay or postpone his anger, which will prevent
him from saying or doing something out of anger which he
would regret later. Other people will praise, honor and highly
regard the person who disregards or overlooks when another
person violates or breaks a law, command or duty.

17. Turns Away Anger

NIV 29:8 Mockers stir up a city, but wise men turn
away anger.

KJV 29:8 Scornful men bring a city into a snare: but
wise men turn away wrath.

AMP 29:8 Scoffers set a city afire [inflaming the minds of
the people], but wise men turn away wrath.

Wise people, that is, people who have sound judgment,
keen discernment and deep understanding, avoid strong,
vengeful anger by using their wisdom to remain quiet, speak
kind words, etc. They will turn away anger in themselves
when it arises, as well as turn away anger when someone is
angry towards them. If we walk in love, anger will not be
allowed to come in.

18. Thinks About and Knows What To Do Before Doing It

NIV 14:8 The wisdom of the prudent is to give thought to

their ways, but the folly of fools is deception.

KJV 14:8   The wisdom of the prudent is to understand his way: but the folly of fools is deceit.

AMP 14:8   The Wisdom [godly Wisdom, which is comprehensive insight into the ways and purposes of God] of the prudent is to understand his way, but the folly of [self-confident] fools is to deceive.

The wisdom of those people who are prudent, who have good judgment and common sense, is to think about and know what they are going to do before they do it. They think about the advantages and disadvantages and what the anticipated result will be of their actions before they do them. However, the folly or lack of good sense or prudence of fools, those who lack good judgment or prudence, is deception. Deception implies imposing a false idea or belief that causes ignorance, bewilderment (to perplex or confuse) or helplessness.

19. Wise Plans

NIV 21:22   A wise man attacks the city of the mighty and pulls down the stronghold in which they trust.

KJV 21:22   A wise man scaleth the city of the mighty, and casteth down the strength of the confidence thereof.

AMP 21:22   A wise man scales the city walls of the mighty and brings down the stronghold in which they trust.

A wise person uses sound judgment, keen discernment and deep understanding to plan his "attack." He knows if he can defeat what they have confidence in, then he will be victorious. In this verse, the wise man "scales" the city of the mighty. To "scale" is to attack with or take by means of scaling ladders. The city walls were what the people inside the city put their confidence in. When the wise man overcame what the people put their confidence in, then it became much easier to "take the city" or to obtain the objective.

20. Has Understanding

NIV 14:33   Wisdom reposes in the heart of the discerning and even among fools she lets herself be known.

KJV 14:33   Wisdom resteth in the heart of him that hath understanding: but that which is in the midst of fools is made known.

AMP 14:33   Wisdom rests [silently] in the mind and heart of him who has understanding, but that which is in the inward part of [self-confident] fools is made known.

Wisdom is present in the person who has understanding and is highly valued. However, with fools, or those who lack good judgment, prudence and understanding, wisdom is not found. Their actions, words and decisions will quickly disclose whether they have wisdom or not.

21. Works Hard

NIV 10:5   He who gathers crops in summer is a wise son, but he who sleeps during harvest is a disgraceful son.

KJV 10:5   He that gathereth in summer is a wise son: but he that sleepeth in harvest is a son that causeth shame.

AMP 10:5   He who gathers in summer is a wise son, but he who sleeps in harvest is a son who causes shame.

A wise son will work hard while he can, while he is able and while opportunity is available.

Proverbs 30:25

NIV 30:25   Ants are creatures of little strength, yet they store up their food in the summer.

KJV 30:25   The ants are a people not strong, yet they prepare their meat in the summer.

AMP 30:25   The ants are a people not strong, yet they lay up their food in the summer.

The ant does not have great physical or intellectual power. It does not have great resources of wealth or talent. (Some people are like this.) However, they work hard and diligently and use their wisdom to store up their food in the summer so that they will have food year round. People should learn from the ant to do the same: work hard, diligently, while you can and save your money so when you cannot earn money you will have enough to live from.

22. Wealth

NIV 14:24   The wealth of the wise is their crown, but the folly of fools yields folly.

KJV 14:24 The crown of the wise is their riches: but the foolishness of fools is folly.

AMP 14:24 The crown of the wise is their wealth of Wisdom, but the foolishness of [self-confident] fools is [nothing but] folly.

A "crown" is a reward of victory or mark of honor. Therefore, the reward of victory or mark of honor of the wise person is their wealth. "Foolishness" implies the character of being or seeming unable to use good judgment, discretion or good sense. "Fools" are people who lack good judgment, prudence and understanding. "Folly" here means an excessively costly or unprofitable undertaking. Therefore, "foolishness" or being unable to use good judgment, discretion or good sense, of people who lack good judgment, prudence and understanding, will lead to an excessively costly or unprofitable undertaking.

Proverbs 21:20

NIV 21:20 In the house of the wise are stores of choice food and oil, but a foolish man devours all he has.

KJV 21:20 There is treasure to be desired and oil in the dwelling of the wise; but a foolish man spendeth it up.

AMP 21:20 There are precious treasures and oil in the dwelling of the wise, but a self-confident and foolish man swallows it up and wastes it.

A wise person invests his money wisely and does not spend it frivolously. Therefore, he will be prosperous and have money in reserve.

23. Favor of Those in Authority Over You

NIV 14:35   A king delights in a wise servant, but a shameful servant incurs his wrath.

KJV 14:35   The king's favour is toward a wise servant: but his wrath is against him that causeth shame.

AMP 14:35   The king's favor is toward a wise and discreet servant, but his wrath is against him who does shamefully.

The word "king" here means one who holds a preeminent position, that is, having paramount rank, dignity or importance. In the days the Old Testament was written, there were kings, such as King Solomon who wrote this verse, who had servants they owned who served them. Some servants were wiser than others. A "wise" servant pleased the king with his ability to discern inner qualities and relationships, knowledge, insight, good sense, good judgment, a wise attitude or course of action. However, a "shameful" servant will incur the king's "wrath." Shame is a condition of humiliating disgrace or brings strong regret. "Wrath" here means anger leading to punishment for an offense or crime, divine chastisement. The word "king" represents God or Jesus Christ and the word "servant" represents all born-again Christians today.

24. A Wise Woman Develops Her Family and Home

NIV 14:1   The wise woman builds her house, but with her own hands the foolish one tears hers down.

KJV 14:1   Every wise woman buildeth her house: but the foolish plucketh it down with her hands.

AMP 14:1   Every wise woman builds her house, but the foolish one tears it down with her own hands.

Every wise woman, that is, every woman who has sound judgment, prudence and understanding, will develop her family and home according to a systematic plan, by a definite process or on a particular base.

25. Spanks and Corrects Their Children and Speaks Kind Words to Them

NIV 29:15   The rod of correction imparts wisdom, but a child left to himself disgraces his mother.

KJV 29:15   The rod and reproof give wisdom: but a child left to himself bringeth his mother to shame.

AMP 29:15 The rod and reproof give wisdom, but a child left undisciplined brings his mother to shame.

The "rod," which was a straight, slender stick or a bundle of twigs used to punish and "reprove," which is to scold or correct usually gently or with kind intent, gives wisdom. Notice, the rod alone does not give wisdom to the child. It must be accompanied with reproof, to correct the child with kind words, to make the child wiser. However, if the rod and reproof are not administered to the child in times when correction is needed, the child will bring the parents shame and disgrace.

26. A Wise Son Listens Carefully to His Father

NIV 13:1   A wise son heeds his father's instruction, but a mocker does not listen to rebuke.

KJV 13:1   A wise son heareth his father's instruction: but a scorner heareth not rebuke.

AMP 13:1   A wise son heeds [and is the fruit of] his father's instruction and correction, but a scoffer listens not to rebuke.

A wise son will listen carefully to his father's instruction.

27. Makes Parents Proud

NIV 15:20   A wise son brings joy to his father, but a foolish man despises his mother.

KJV 15:20   A wise son maketh a glad father: but a foolish man despiseth his mother.

AMP 15:20   A wise son makes a glad father, but a self-confident and foolish man despises his mother and puts her to shame.

A wise son who uses sound judgment, has keen discernment and deep understanding, makes his father very proud and happy.

Proverbs 29:3

NIV 29:3   A man who loves wisdom brings joy to his father, but a companion of prostitutes squanders his wealth.

KJV 29:3   Whoso loveth wisdom rejoiceth his father: but he that keepeth company with harlots spendeth his substance.

AMP 29:3   Whoever loves skillful and godly Wisdom rejoices his father, but he who associates with harlots wastes his substance.

A person who loves and operates in wisdom daily makes his father happy and proud, while he who visits prostitutes squanders, or wastes, his money.

28. Overcomes Disadvantages

NIV 30:26   coneys are creatures of little power, yet they make their home in the crags;

KJV 30:26   The conies are but a feeble folk, yet they make their houses in the rocks;

AMP 30:26   The conies are but a feeble folk, yet they make their houses in the rocks;

The conies are European rabbits. They are feeble, that is, they are weak, lacking in strength. However, they are very wise in that they make their homes where they live among the rocky cliffs so that other more powerful animals cannot get to them. Although some people may feel like they are at a disadvantage, if they use wisdom, they can "overcome the disadvantage" and not allow "it" to keep them from succeeding.

29. Has Self-Discipline and Initiative

NIV 30:27   locusts have no king, yet they advance together in ranks;

KJV 30:27   The locusts have no king, yet go they forth all of them by bands;

AMP 30:27   The locusts have no king, yet they go forth all of them by bands;

The locusts are good examples of "self-discipline" and

"initiative." Although they do not have a leader instructing them where to line up and fly, they all line up by using self-discipline to fill in where there is a gap until they are all united for a common purpose. We too should be wise by using self-discipline and taking the initiative.

30. Determined

NIV 30:28   a lizard can be caught with the hand, yet it is found in kings' palaces.

KJV 30:28   The spider taketh hold with her hands, and is in kings' palaces.

AMP 30:28   The lizard you can seize with your hands, yet it is in kings' palaces.

The spider may not have the most "opportunity" to be successful. However, by "choice and determination," it can be very successful and by wisely using its legs to hold onto surfaces, it can live in kings' palaces. Instead of complaining, making excuses and blaming others for our circumstances, if we are wise in the decisions that we make and are determined to be successful, we can be very successful.

31. Chooses Not To Be Around Sin, Wickedness, Bad Character or Conduct

NIV 14:16   A wise man fears the LORD and shuns evil, but a fool is hotheaded and reckless.

KJV 14:16   A wise man feareth, and departeth from evil: but the fool rageth, and is confident.

AMP 14:16   A wise man suspects danger and cautiously

avoids evil, but the fool bears himself insolently and is [presumptuously] confident.

A wise person will anticipate or will be aware of danger and will
leave when he is around sin, wickedness, bad character or conduct.
However, a fool gets extremely angry and is arrogant.

32. Opposes the Wicked

NIV 20:26 A wise king winnows out the wicked; he
drives the threshing wheel over them.

KJV 20:26 A wise king scattereth the wicked, and bringeth the wheel over them.

AMP 20:26 A wise king winnows out the wicked [from
among the good] and brings the threshing
wheel over them [to separate the chaff from
the grain].

A wise king will remove from society people who are wicked, that is, people who are morally very bad, evil, causing or
likely to cause harm, distress or trouble. He will hold them
accountable to the full extent of the law and enforce the appro-
priate punishment. He is "wise" because if he does not, the evil
people's actions will bring undeserving harm to the people who
are law-abiding citizens. These law-abiding citizens will respect
and honor him for his wise actions. The word "king" here can
also be thought of as "someone in a position of authority."

33. Hates Wickedness

NIV 8:7 My mouth speaks what is true, for my lips
detest wickedness.

KJV 8:7   For my mouth shall speak truth; and wickedness is an abomination to my lips.

AMP 8:7   For my mouth shall utter truth, and wrongdoing is detestable and loathsome to my lips.

Wisdom's words are true. Wisdom hates the morally bad, deceptive, evil words and actions of wickedness.

34. Strengthened By Using Wisdom Consistently

NIV 24:3   By wisdom a house is built, and through understanding it is established;

KJV 24:3   Through wisdom is an house builded; and by understanding it is established:

AMP 24:3   Through skillful and godly Wisdom is a house (a life, a home, a family) built, and by understanding it is established [on a sound and good foundation],

Our bodies are the "temple" of the Holy Spirit. As we obtain wisdom, wisdom becomes the foundation for all that we say and do. We become strengthened or more developed, more mature as we gain understanding through God revealing it to us.

35. Uses Wisdom Daily

NIV 28:26   He who trusts in himself is a fool, but he who walks in wisdom is kept safe.

KJV 28:26   He that trusteth in his own heart is a fool: but whoso walketh wisely, he shall be delivered.

AMP 28:26   He who leans on, trusts in, and is confident

of his own mind and heart is a [self-confi-
dent] fool, but he who walks in skillful and
godly Wisdom shall be delivered.

The person who only does what he thinks is a fool, but the
person who lives every day, making wise decisions, shall be set
free. This implies that the person who "walks" in wisdom daily
trusts in something other than his own ability. This something
is the God-given wisdom.

36. Gets Satisfaction or Gratification
    By Having and Using Wisdom

NIV 10:23 A fool finds pleasure in evil conduct, but a
man of understanding delights in wisdom.

KJV 10:23 It is as sport to a fool to do mischief: but a
man of understanding hath wisdom.

AMP 10:23 It is as sport to a [self-confident] fool to do
wickedness, but to have skillful and godly
Wisdom is pleasure and relaxation to a man
of understanding.

A fool, that is, a person lacking good judgment, prudence and
understanding, enjoys doing wrong and displaying mean behavior. A person who has understanding gets extreme satisfaction or
a high degree of gratification by having and using wisdom in the
words they speak, decisions they make and actions they take.

37. Keeps His Focus and Attention on Wisdom

NIV 17:24 A discerning man keeps wisdom in view, but a
fool's eyes wander to the ends of the earth.

KJV 17:24 Wisdom is before him that hath understanding; but the eyes of a fool are in the ends of the earth.

AMP 17:24 A man of understanding sets skillful and godly Wisdom before his face, but the eyes of a [self-confident] fool are on the ends of the earth.

The person who has obtained understanding keeps his focus and attention on wisdom, always striving to become even wiser. However, a fool, or a person who lacks good judgment, prudence and understanding, has his attention on other things that are useless to him.

F. Wisdom's Instructions to Us

1. Reverence God

NIV 15:33 The fear of the LORD teaches a man wisdom, and humility comes before honor.

KJV 15:33 The fear of the LORD is the instruction of wisdom; and before honour is humility.

AMP 15:33 The reverent and worshipful fear of the Lord brings instruction in Wisdom, and humility comes before honor.

The respect and reverence for God are what wisdom instructs or teaches us to do. We must humble ourselves before God and man before God will bless us with honor among other people.

2. Humble Ourselves

NIV 3:7   Do not be wise in your own eyes; fear the LORD and shun evil.

KJV 3:7   Be not wise in thine own eyes; fear the LORD, and depart from evil.

AMP 3:7   Be not wise in your own eyes; reverently fear and worship the Lord and turn [entirely] away from evil.

We are to be humble with the wisdom God has given us and not to think we are "better than someone else" just because we have more wisdom. Instead, reverence and honor the Lord and do not do anything evil.

3. Meditate Upon Wisdom's Instruction

NIV 3:1   My son, do not forget my teaching, but keep my commands in your heart,

KJV 3:1   My son, forget not my law; but let thine heart keep my commandments:

AMP 3:1   My son, forget not my law or teaching, but let your heart keep my commandments;

Wisdom says for us to not forget what wisdom has taught us, but to meditate upon and memorize wisdom's commands until they are in our heart permanently.

Proverbs 4:5

NIV 4:5   Get wisdom, get understanding; do not forget my words or swerve from them.

KJV 4:5   Get wisdom, get understanding: forget it not; neither decline from the words of my mouth.

AMP 4:5   Get skillful and godly Wisdom, get understanding (discernment, comprehension, and interpretation); do not forget and do not turn back from the words of my mouth.

We are instructed to "get" wisdom and understanding, read God's Word, study, meditate, memorize it, ask God to give us wisdom. Once we "get" wisdom and understanding, we must continue to meditate upon and speak wisdom's teachings so that we will not forget them or stop obeying wisdom's commands.

NIV 4:21   Do not let them out of your sight, keep them within your heart;

KJV 4:21   Let them not depart from thine eyes; keep them in the midst of thine heart.

AMP 4:21   Let them not depart from your sight; keep them in the center of your heart.

We are to continually and consistently read and think about wisdom's sayings, keeping them in our hearts and minds.

4. Listen to Wisdom and Do as Instructed

NIV 4:20   My son, pay attention to what I say; listen closely to my words.

KJV 4:20   My son, attend to my words; incline thine ear unto my sayings.

AMP 4:20   My son, attend to my words; consent and submit to my sayings.

We are to pay close attention to and think about wisdom's words. We are to lean, tend or become drawn towards the course of conduct that wisdom's sayings teach.

Proverbs 8:32

NIV 8:32 Now then, my sons, listen to me; blessed are those who keep my ways.

KJV 8:32 Now therefore hearken unto me, O ye children: for blessed are they that keep my ways.

AMP 8:32 Now therefore listen to me, O you sons; for blessed (happy, fortunate, to be envied) are those who keep my ways.

So therefore, listen carefully to wisdom; blessed are those people who do as wisdom instructs. We are instructed to "listen" to wisdom because those who "keep" wisdom's ways will be blessed. Listening is the first step, but we must also do what wisdom teaches us in order to be blessed.

Proverbs 8:33

NIV 8:33 Listen to my instruction and be wise; do not ignore it.

KJV 8:33 Hear instruction, and be wise, and refuse it not.

AMP 8:33 Hear instruction and be wise, and do not refuse or neglect it.

Listen to wisdom's instruction and be wise; do not ignore it.

Proverbs 22:17

NIV 22:17   Pay attention and listen to the sayings of the wise; apply your heart to what I teach,

KJV 22:17   Bow down thine ear, and hear the words of the wise, and apply thine heart unto my knowledge.

AMP 22:17   Listen (consent and submit) to the words of the wise, and apply your mind to my knowledge;

We are to listen carefully to the words of the wise person and to study and think about the knowledge of the wise person until we know and understand it in our own hearts and minds. For it is pleasing when we keep the words of the wise in our heart and have them available and ready to speak at any time.

Proverbs 23:26

NIV 23:26   My son, give me your heart and let your eyes keep to my ways,

KJV 23:26   My son, give me thine heart, and let thine eyes observe my ways.

AMP 23:26   My son, give me your heart and let your eyes observe and delight in my ways,

We are to sincerely give our hearts to wisdom. That is, we must listen to and do everything wisdom instructs us to do. Our focus and attention are to be on wisdom's ways.

5. Wise Action

NIV 9:8   Do not rebuke a mocker or he will hate you; rebuke a wise man and he will love you.

KJV 9:8   Reprove not a scorner, lest he hate thee: rebuke a wise man, and he will love thee.

AMP 9:8   Reprove not a scorner, lest he hate you; reprove a wise man, and he will love you.

"Reprove" implies an often kindly intent to correct a fault. A scorner is a person who frequently expresses open dislike and disrespect or derision (an object of ridicule or scorn), often mixed with indignation (anger aroused by something unjust, unworthy or mean). Therefore, we are instructed not to attempt to kindly correct a person who is consistently angry, expressing their dislike and disrespect for others and who ridicules others because it will be useless and only make the scorner hate us. However, if we rebuke, that is to criticize sharply or reprimand a wise person, he will respond to us by loving us.

6. Hang Around Wise People

NIV 13:20   He who walks with the wise grows wise, but a companion of fools suffers harm.

KJV 13:20   He that walketh with wise men shall be wise: but a companion of fools shall be destroyed.

AMP 13:20   He who walks [as a companion] with wise men is wise, but he who associates with [self-confident] fools is [a fool himself and] shall smart for it.

A person who associates with and spends their time with wise people shall become wise himself, but a person who hangs around other people who are fools, that is, they lack good judgment, prudence and knowledge, shall be destroyed, or torn down, causing destruction in all areas of life.

7. Work

NIV 6:6-8   Go to the ant, you sluggard; consider its ways and be wise! It has no commander, no overseer or ruler, yet it stores its provisions in summer and gathers its food at harvest.

KJV 6:6-8   Go to the ant, thou sluggard; consider her ways, and be wise: Which having no guide, overseer, or ruler, provideth her meat in the summer, and gathereth her food in the harvest.

AMP 6:6-8   Go to the ant, you sluggard; consider her ways and be wise! Which, having no chief, overseer, or ruler, provides her food in the summer and gathers her supplies in the harvest.

The sluggard, that is, an habitually lazy person, is instructed to be wise by observing the ant and learning how important it is to work. The ant has no boss or anyone making it work, yet it knows that it must work hard all summer to store up food for the winter.

Proverbs 23:4

NIV 23:4   Do not wear yourself out to get rich; have the wisdom to show restraint.

KJV 23:4   Labour not to be rich: cease from thine own wisdom.

AMP 23:4 Weary not yourself to be rich; cease from your own [human] wisdom.

When we work, we are not to have the primary goal of becoming rich. We are commanded to stop striving to become rich through our own human efforts. Our primary goal is to seek first the kingdom of God and then all these things shall be added unto us. God will bless us tremendously if we put Him and His work first in our lives.

8. Be Fair in Judging

NIV 24:23 These also are sayings of the wise: To show partiality in judging is not good.

KJV 24:23 These things also belong to the wise. It is not good to have respect of persons in judgment.

AMP 24:23 These also are sayings of the wise: To discriminate and show partiality, having respect of persons in judging, is not good.

We should always be fair and impartial when we are in a position of judging others, as rich blessings will come our way if we are.

9. Children

NIV 23:19 Listen, my son, and be wise, and keep your heart on the right path.

KJV 23:19 Hear thou, my son, and be wise, and guide thine heart in the way.

AMP 23:19 Hear, my son, and be wise, and direct your mind in the way [of the Lord].

Children are being instructed to be wise and to be careful to guide their heart in the right way. That is, to guard what their eyes see and what their ears hear since what goes into their minds will go into their hearts and what is in their hearts will come out of their mouth.

10. Make Your Parents Proud

NIV 27:11   Be wise, my son, and bring joy to my heart; then I can answer anyone who treats me with contempt.

KJV 27:11   My son, be wise, and make my heart glad, that I may answer him that reproacheth me.

AMP 27:11   My son, be wise, and make my heart glad, that I may answer him who reproaches me [as having failed in my parental duty].

We are instructed to "be wise." If we are wise, we will make our parents proud and happy. If a person mildly scolds our parents because of something we are being accused of doing, our parents can confidently defend us because they know we "are wise" and what we would do in certain situations.

11. Do Not Attempt to Teach Fools Wisdom's Ways

NIV 23:9   Do not speak to a fool, for he will scorn the wisdom of your words.

KJV 23:9   Speak not in the ears of a fool: for he will despise the wisdom of thy words.

AMP 23:9   Speak not in the ears of a [self-confident]

fool, for he will despise the [godly] Wisdom of your words.

We are instructed not to attempt to teach wisdom's ways to a fool, that is, a person lacking in good judgment, prudence or understanding, because he will strongly dislike or even hate the wisdom of your words.

Proverbs 29:9

NIV 29:9   If a wise man goes to court with a fool, the fool rages and scoffs, and there is no peace.

KJV 29:9   If a wise man contendeth with a foolish man, whether he rage or laugh, there is no rest.

AMP 29:9   If a wise man has an argument with a foolish man, the fool only rages or laughs, and there is no rest.

If a wise person argues or debates with a foolish man, there will be no peace of mind or spirit, regardless of whether the wise person displays violent and uncontrolled anger or laughter.

G. What Having Wisdom Will Do for You

1. What We Must Do

NIV 2:1-2   My son, if you accept my words and store up my commands within you, turning your ear to wisdom and applying your heart to under-standing.

KJV 2:1-2   My son, if thou wilt receive my words, and hide my commandments with thee; so that thou incline thine ear unto wisdom, and apply thine heart unto understanding;

AMP 2:1-2 My son, if you will receive my words and treasure up my commandments within you, making your ear attentive to skillful and godly Wisdom and inclining and directing your heart and mind to understanding [applying all your powers to the quest for it];

There are conditions here. If we accept wisdom's advice and memorize and meditate upon wisdom's commands until we know them, in order for us to listen intently to wisdom's words, we will sincerely and earnestly strive to thoroughly understand.

2. Safety and Peace

NIV 1:33 but whoever listens to me will live in safety and be at ease, without fear of harm.

KJV 1:33 But whoso hearkeneth unto me shall dwell safely, and shall be quiet from fear of evil.

AMP 1:33 But whoso hearkens to me [Wisdom] shall dwell securely and in confident trust and shall be quiet, without fear or dread of evil.

Whoever listens to wise advice will live in safety and peace, without the fear of being harmed.

3. Happiness, Joy and Peace

NIV 3:17 Her ways are pleasant ways, and all her paths are peace.

KJV 3:17   Her ways are ways of pleasantness, and all her paths are peace.

AMP 3:17   Her ways are highways of pleasantness, and all her paths are peace.

Our daily lives will be full of happiness, joy and peace when we use what wisdom has taught us.

4. Protection

NIV 2:12   Wisdom will save you from the ways of wicked men, from men whose words are perverse,

KJV 2:12   To deliver thee from the way of the evil man, from the man that speaketh froward things;

AMP 2:12   To deliver you from the way of evil and the evil men, from men who speak perverse things and are liars,

Wisdom will protect you from the ways and perverse words of evil people who attempt to harm you in one way or another.

Proverbs 2:13

NIV 2:13   who leave the straight paths to walk in dark ways,

KJV 2:13   Who leave the paths of uprightness, to walk in the ways of darkness;

AMP 2:13   Men who forsake the paths of uprightness to walk in the ways of darkness,

These evil people are people who have chosen to do evil rather than choosing to do good.

Proverbs 2:14

NIV 2:14   who delight in doing wrong and rejoice in the perverseness of evil,

KJV 2:14   Who rejoice to do evil, and delight in the frowardness of the wicked;

AMP 2:14   Who rejoice to do evil and delight in the perverseness of evil,

These evil people actually enjoy doing wrong and are happy when they see the perverse results of their actions.

Proverbs 2:15

NIV 2:15   whose paths are crooked and who are devious in their ways

KJV 2:15   Whose ways are crooked, and they froward in their paths:

AMP 2:15   Who are crooked in their ways, wayward and devious in their paths.

These evil people's ways are dishonest and they are habitually disobedient and opposing in their actions and words.

Proverbs 4:6

NIV 4:6   Do not forsake wisdom, and she will protect you; love her, and she will watch over you.

KJV 4:6   Forsake her not, and she shall preserve thee: love her, and she shall keep thee.

AMP 4:6   Forsake not [Wisdom], and she will keep, defend, and protect you; love her, and she will guard you.

If we do not abandon and forget what wisdom has taught us, then it will protect us. If we highly regard and cherish wisdom, it will take care of us in all areas of our life.

Proverbs 14:3

NIV 14:3   A fool's talk brings a rod to his back, but the lips of the wise protect them.

KJV 14:3   In the mouth of the foolish is a rod of pride: but the lips of the wise shall preserve them.

AMP 14:3   In the fool's own mouth is a rod [to shame] his pride, but the wise men's lips preserve them.

"Pride" here suggests an assumed superiority or loftiness, even being arrogant, which implies a claiming for oneself of more consideration or importance than is warranted. In other words, thinking more highly of oneself than they should. A "rod" was a straight, slender stick or a bundle of twigs used to punish. The "foolish" person is one who lacks good judgment, prudence and understanding. Therefore, the foolish person will be punished because of the prideful, arrogant words that he speaks. However, the words of the wise will protect them, keeping them safe from injury, harm or destruction.

5. Our Thoughts and Emotions Will Be Pleasant

NIV 2:10   For wisdom will enter your heart, and knowledge will be pleasant to your soul.

KJV 2:10   When wisdom entereth into thine heart, and knowledge is pleasant unto thy soul;

AMP 2:10   For skillful and godly Wisdom shall enter into your heart, and knowledge shall be pleasant to you.

When wisdom enters our heart, knowledge will cause our soul (mind and emotions) to be pleasant (pleasant thoughts and emotions).   We obtain wisdom, knowledge and understanding from God's Word and through the Holy Spirit.

6. Your Mind and Emotions Will Benefit

NIV 24:13-14   Eat honey, my son, for it is good; honey from the comb is sweet to your taste. Know also that wisdom is sweet to your soul; if you find it, there is a future hope for you, and your hope will not be cut off.

KJV 24:13-14   My son, eat thou honey, because it is good; and the honeycomb, which is sweet to thy taste: So shall the knowledge of wisdom be unto thy soul: when thou hast found it, then there shall be a reward, and thy expectation shall not be cut off.

AMP 24:13-14   My son, eat honey, because it is good, and the drippings of the honeycomb are sweet to your taste. So shall you know skillful and godly Wisdom to be thus to your life; if you find it, then shall there be a future and a reward, and your hope and expectation shall not be cut off.

Just as honey is good for your body and is sweet to your taste, so shall the knowledge that you will have when you get wisdom, be unto your soul. In other words, the knowledge that comes with wisdom will be good for your mind and emotions, as well as make you feel good, strengthening your confidence and self-esteem. When you have found it (notice you must "find it"), then there shall be a reward. The knowledge of wisdom shall serve you well in all areas of life. You will not be disappointed in what you had expected, as it will be well worth the time and effort it took to obtain it.

7. Life and Health to Your Body, Mind and Soul

NIV 4:22   for they are life to those who find them and health to a man's whole body.

KJV 4:22   For they are life unto those that find them, and health to all their flesh.

AMP 4:22   For they are life to those who find them, healing and health to all their flesh.

For wisdom's sayings bring life to those who do what it takes to find them, that is, to read and study God's Word, and health to all of their body, mind and soul.

8. Long Life, Riches and Honor

NIV 3:16   Long life is in her right hand; in her left hand are riches and honor.

KJV 3:16   Length of days is in her right hand; and in her left hand riches and honour.

AMP 3:16   Length of days is in her right hand, and in

her left hand are riches and honor.

The rewards that come with having wisdom are long life and riches and honor. We will live a long time on this earth, be wealthy and be honored by people when we have wisdom.

9. Praise, Honor and Distinction

NIV 3:35   The wise inherit honor, but fools he holds up to shame.

KJV 3:35   The wise shall inherit glory: but shame shall be the promotion of fools.

AMP 3:35   The wise shall inherit glory (all honor and good) but shame is the highest rank conferred on [self-confident] fools.

Wise people shall "inherit" "glory." The word "inherit" means to come into possession of or receive especially as a right or divine portion. The word "glory" means praise, honor or distinction given by common consent. Therefore, we can say, people who walk daily in wisdom shall receive praise, honor and distinction from people. Fools, or people lacking good judgment, prudence and understanding, shall feel shame, a painful emotion caused by consciousness or guilt; humiliating disgrace, bringing strong regret.

10. You Will Be Successful, Promoted, Honored, Prosperous and Wise

NIV 4:8   Esteem her, and she will exalt you; embrace her, and she will honor you.

KJV 4:8   Exalt her, and she shall promote thee: she shall bring thee to honour, when thou dost embrace her.

AMP 4:8   Prize Wisdom highly and exalt her, and she will exalt and promote you; she will bring you to honor when you embrace her.

When we have wisdom, it will cause us to be successful, promoted, honored, prosperous and wise in all that we say and do. Every decision we make we will use discretion and make the best decision.

11. Dignity and Honor By Others

NIV 4:9   She will set a garland of grace on your head and present you with a crown of splendor.

KJV 4:9   She shall give to thine head an ornament of grace: a crown of glory shall she deliver to thee.

AMP 4:9   She shall give to your head a wreath of gracefulness; a crown of beauty and glory will she deliver to you.

Having wisdom will bless us by being adorned or embellished with dignity and honor by others. Wisdom will exalt or elevate us to an excellence, reaching the highest conceivable degree.

12. You Will Be Complimented and Praised

NIV 12:8   A man is praised according to his wisdom, but men with warped minds are despised.

KJV 12:8   A man shall be commended according to his

wisdom: but he that is of a perverse heart shall be despised.

AMP 12:8   A man shall be commended according to his Wisdom [godly Wisdom, which is comprehensive insight into the ways and purposes of God], but he who is of a perverse heart shall be despised.

A person will be complimented and praised according to how much wisdom he or she has, but the person whose heart has turned away from what is right or good shall be despised or strongly disliked.

13. Strength

NIV 24:5   A wise man has great power, and a man of knowledge increases strength;

KJV 24:5   A wise man is strong; yea, a man of knowledge increaseth strength.

AMP 24:5   A wise man is strong and is better than a strong man, and a man of knowledge increases and strenghtens his power;

A wise man is "strong" because by possessing sound judgment, keen discernment and deep understanding, he has what it takes to be successful in everything he attempts to do. A man of knowledge or a man who possesses the knowledge that only God can give "increases his strength" by continuing to get more knowledge. At such times when he needs it, the knowledge and wisdom are there for him to be able to make wise decisions, which will bring him success.

14. Your Parents Will Be Proud of You

NIV 10:1   The proverbs of Solomon: A wise son brings
            joy to his father, but a foolish son grief to his
            mother.

KJV 10:1   The proverbs of Solomon. A wise son maketh
            a glad father: but a foolish son is the heaviness
            of his mother.

AMP 10:1   The Proverbs of Solomon: A wise son makes
            a glad father, but a foolish and self-confident
            son is the grief of his mother.

A child who becomes wise as he or she grows up makes his
or her parents proud and happy.

Proverbs 23:15

NIV 23:15   My son, if your heart is wise, then my heart
            will be glad;

KJV 23:15   My son, if thine heart be wise, my heart shall
            rejoice, even mine.

AMP 23:15   My son, if your heart is wise, my heart will be
            glad, even mine;

If a child becomes wise, that is, if the child uses sound
judgment, has keen discernment and deep understanding, it
will bring joy to the parents.

Proverbs 23:24

NIV 23:24   The father of a righteous man has great joy;

he who has a wise son delights in him.

KJV 23:24 The father of the righteous shall greatly re-joice: and he that begetteth a wise child shall have joy of him.

AMP 23:24 The father of the [uncompromisingly] righteous (the upright, in right standing with God) shall greatly rejoice, and he who becomes the father of a wise child shall have joy in him.

The "righteous," those people who are free from sin, acting in accord with divine law, shall cause their father to greatly rejoice. The father who produces a wise child as an outgrowth from himself shall be proud of him or her and he or she will bring the father joy.

Proverbs 27:11

NIV 27:11 Be wise, my son, and bring joy to my heart; then I can answer anyone who treats me with contempt.

KJV 27:11 My son, be wise, and make my heart glad, that I may answer him that reproacheth me.

AMP 27:11 My son, be wise, and make my heart glad, that I may answer him who reproaches me [as having failed in my parental duty].

We are instructed to "be wise." If we are wise, we will make our parents proud and happy. If a person mildly scolds our parents because of something we are being accused of doing, our parents can confidently defend us because they know we "are wise" and what we would do in certain situations.

15. God Will Be on Your Side

NIV 21:30   There is no wisdom, no insight, no plan that can succeed against the LORD.

KJV 21:30   There is no wisdom nor understanding nor counsel against the LORD.

AMP 21:30 There is no [human] wisdom or understanding or counsel [that can prevail] against the Lord.

Being an "upright" person and following God will cause God to be on your side. No plans or strategies of wicked people will succeed against God. The victory will rest with God.

16. Life and Favor of God

NIV 8:35   For whoever finds me finds life and receives favor from the LORD.

KJV 8:35   For whoso findeth me findeth life, and shall obtain favour of the LORD.

AMP 8:35   For whoever finds me [Wisdom] finds life and draws forth and obtains favor from the Lord.

Whoever "finds" wisdom, finds life. Notice, we have to "find" wisdom. We "find" wisdom by doing what is required, that is, to study God's Word. God will then give us wisdom. Also, if we find wisdom, we will receive favor from God.

17. Promotion, Financial Blessing and Favor of Men

NIV 17:2   A wise servant will rule over a disgraceful son, and will share the inheritance as one of the brothers.

KJV 17:2   A wise servant shall have rule over a son that causeth shame, and shall have part of the inheritance among the brethren.

AMP 17:2   A wise servant shall have rule over a son who causes shame, and shall share in the inheritance among the brothers.

A wise servant, that is, a person who performs duties for the person or around the home of a master or personal employer, who does so by using good, sound judgment, keen discernment and deep understanding will have authority or control over a son who causes shame, something that brings humiliating disgrace and strong regret, to his parents. Not only will the wise servant rule over the son who brings shame, but he will also share in the inheritance along with the children. He will gain favor by doing his work well with a humble attitude.

18. Riches, Honor, Enduring Wealth and Righteousness

NIV 8:18   With me are riches and honor, enduring wealth and prosperity.

KJV 8:18   Riches and honour are with me; yea, durable riches and righteousness.

AMP 8:18   Riches and honor are with me, enduring wealth and righteousness (uprightness in every area and relation, and right standing with God).

With wisdom comes riches, honor, enduring wealth and righteousness. Notice, not only will those who have wisdom become prosperous, but their prosperity or wealth will be enduring. In other words, they will not lose their wealth, but will continue to get wealthier. They will be honored by others and will have righteousness.

19. Choose Wisdom Rather Than Money

NIV 8:10   Choose my instruction instead of silver, knowledge rather than choice gold,

KJV 8:10   Receive my instruction, and not silver; and knowledge rather than choice gold.

AMP 8:10   Receive my instruction in preference to [striving for] silver, and knowledge rather than choice gold,

We have a choice. The "wise choice" is to "choose" wisdom's instruction and knowledge rather than chasing wealth. The point being made is having wisdom and knowledge are the most important things you can have, more important than having money. The reason is that if we have wisdom and knowledge, we will have the ability to get wealth as well as many other blessings: honor and long, healthy life, happiness and much more. God wants our focus, attention and motive to be on knowing, speaking and doing His Word, to spread His gospel to other people, discipling or teaching them about His goodness and power.

20. Wisdom Is the Most Valuable

NIV 8:11   for wisdom is more precious than rubies, and nothing you desire can compare with her.

KJV 8:11   For wisdom is better than rubies; and all the things that may be desired are not to be compared to it.

AMP 8:11 For skillful and godly Wisdom is better than rubies or pearls, and all the things that may be desired are not to be compared to it.

Wisdom is far more valuable to us than anything that has monetary value. All the "things" we desire to have are not to be compared to having wisdom.

21. Wisdom Is More Valuable Than Money

NIV 16:16 How much better to get wisdom than gold, to choose understanding rather than silver!

KJV 16:16 How much better is it to get wisdom than gold! and to get understanding rather to be chosen than silver!

AMP 16:16 How much better it is to get skillful and godly Wisdom than gold! And to get understanding is to be chosen rather than silver.

It is much better to "get" wisdom and understanding than it is to get a lot of money. The reasons are if we have wisdom and understanding, we will make wise decisions in all areas of life, which will cause all areas of our life to be successful including our finances. Additionally, once we have obtained finances, we will have the wisdom to be able to make responsible decisions to keep and grow the wealth God has blessed us with.

Proverbs 8:19

NIV 8:19   My fruit is better than fine gold; what I yield surpasses choice silver.

KJV 8:19   My fruit is better than gold, yea, than fine gold; and my revenue than choice silver.

AMP 8:19   My fruit is better than gold, yes, than refined gold, and my increase than choice silver.

Wisdom's "fruit," or the results we will get by having wisdom, is more "valuable" to us than pure gold. Wisdom's revenue or what money we will get by having wisdom, is better than the finest silver.

Proverbs 3:14

NIV 3:14   for she is more profitable than silver and yields better returns than gold.

KJV 3:14   For the merchandise of it is better than the merchandise of silver, and the gain thereof than fine gold.

AMP 3:14   For the gaining of it is better than the gaining of silver, and the profit of it better than fine gold.

Wisdom will be more valuable and beneficial to us than

having money. Wisdom will actually provide us a much better return. We can use wisdom in all areas of life.

22. Prudence and Financial Blessings

NIV 8:12   I, wisdom, dwell together with prudence; I possess knowledge and discretion.

KJV 8:12   I wisdom dwell with prudence, and find out knowledge of witty inventions.

AMP 8:12   I, Wisdom [from God], make prudence my dwelling, and I find out knowledge and discretion.

When we have wisdom, we will also have prudence or good judgment and common sense. Wisdom will "find out" knowledge of "witty" inventions, which means inventions which are ingeniously clever in conception. Notice, wisdom that is given to us by God when we study and meditate on His Word, will "reveal" or give us ideas which can bring us financial blessings.

23. Ability to Make Wise Decisions

NIV 4:11   I guide you in the way of wisdom and lead you along straight paths.

KJV 4:11   I have taught thee in the way of wisdom; I have led thee in right paths.

AMP 4:11   I have taught you in the way of skillful and godly Wisdom [which is comprehensive insight into the ways and purposes of God]; I have led you in paths of uprightness.

Wisdom and being wise is "a way," a particular way of life, that will keep us from making bad decisions that would cause us heartache, cost us financially, destroy our marriage and family and eventually bring us to ruin.

24. Life Made Easier

NIV 4:12　When you walk, your steps will not be hampered; when you run, you will not stumble.

KJV 4:12　When thou goest, thy steps shall not be straitened; and when thou runnest, thou shalt not stumble.

AMP 4:12　When you walk, your steps shall not be hampered [your path will be clear and open]; and when you run, you shall not stumble.

During our daily lives, what we are attempting to do and accomplish will not be hampered or made difficult with obstacles or problems when we have wisdom. As we begin to have success in what we are attempting to do, we will not fail and we will not have setbacks due to poor decisions.

25. You Will Benefit in All Areas of Life

NIV 9:12　If you are wise, your wisdom will reward you; if you are a mocker, you alone will suffer.

KJV 9:12　If thou be wise, thou shalt be wise for thyself: but if thou scornest, thou alone shalt bear it.

AMP 9:12　If you are wise, you are wise for yourself; if you scorn, you alone will bear it and pay the penalty.

If you are wise, that is, if you have become wise, your wisdom that you have will benefit you in all areas of life. Every decision you make will be made with discretion. The results of one wise decision after another, over a period of time, will provide you with blessings. If you "despise" wisdom, you will be the one to suffer the consequences. The word "despise" means an abrupt rejection or dismissal, to regard as negligible or unimportant.

Proverbs 19:8

NIV 19:8   He who gets wisdom loves his own soul; he who cherishes understanding prospers.

KJV 19:8   He that getteth wisdom loveth his own soul: he that keepeth understanding shall find good.

AMP 19:8   He who gains Wisdom loves his own life; he who keeps understanding shall prosper and find good.

A person who gets or acquires wisdom by doing what is required of him, that is, to seek God by studying His Word and praying, wants to become wise in all that he says and does. Those who desire to gain more and more understanding and are willing to put forth the effort to gain it by studying, meditating or pondering on His Word and praying, will prosper, not only financially, but in all areas of their life.

H. What Happens If Someone Rejects Wisdom?

1. Wisdom Will Not Be Available When They Need It

NIV 1:23-25   If you had responded to my rebuke, I would have poured out my heart to you and made my thoughts known to you. But since you rejected me when I called and no one gave heed when I stretched out my hand, since you ignored all my advice and would not accept my rebuke,

KJV 1:23-25   Turn you at my reproof: behold, I will pour out my spirit unto you, I will make known my words unto you. Because I have called, and ye refused; I have stretched out my hand, and no man regarded; but ye have set at nought all my counsel, and would none of my reproof:

AMP 1:23-25   If you turn (repent) and give heed to my reproof, behold, I [Wisdom] will pour out my spirit upon you, I will make my words known to you. Because I have called and you have refused [to answer], have stretched out my hand and no man has heeded it, and you treated as nothing all my counsel and would accept none of my reproof,

If these "simple" ones, "mockers" and "fools" had listened to wisdom and its correction when it was presented to them, they too could have become wise. However, since they refused to listen to wisdom when it was offered to them and since they ignored all of wisdom's advice and chose not to accept wisdom's correction, when disaster (unforeseen misfortune that ruins), calamity (deep distress or misery), distress (great physical or mental strain and stress) and trouble overwhelm them, they will be on their own, helpless to overcome those problems.

Proverbs 1:26-28

NIV 1:26-28   I in turn will laugh at your disaster; I will mock when calamity overtakes you—when calamity overtakes you like a storm, when disaster sweeps over you like a whirlwind, when distress and trouble overwhelm you. Then they will call to me but I will not answer; they will look for me but will not find me

KJV 1:26-28   I also will laugh at your calamity; I will mock when your fear cometh; when your fear cometh as desolation, and your destruction cometh as a whirlwind; when distress and anguish cometh upon you. Then shall they call upon me, but I will not answer; they shall seek me early, but they shall not find me:

AMP 1:26-28   I also will laugh at your calamity; I will mock when the thing comes that shall cause you terror and panic—When your panic comes as a storm and desolation and your calamity comes on as a whirlwind, when distress and anguish come upon you. Then will they call upon me [Wisdom] but I will not answer; they will seek me early and diligently but they will not find me.

Then they will wish they had wisdom. They will look for wisdom, but they will not find it. It will be too late. They will have to suffer the consequences.

2. They Will Suffer the Consequences

NIV 1:29-30 Since they hated knowledge and did not choose to fear the LORD, since they would not accept my advice and spurned my rebuke,

KJV 1:29-30 For that they hated knowledge, and did not choose the fear of the LORD: They would none of my counsel: they despised all my reproof:

AMP 1:29-30 Because they hated knowledge and did not choose the reverent and worshipful fear of the Lord, would accept none of my counsel, and despised all my reproof,

Since they did not care about obtaining knowledge, chose not to respect and honor God, would not listen to or accept wise advice and rejected wise correction, they will suffer the consequences of their actions and decisions.

Proverbs 1:31-32

NIV 1:31-32 they will eat the fruit of their ways and be filled with the fruit of their schemes. For the waywardness of the simple will kill them, and the complacency of fools will destroy them;

KJV 1:31-32 Therefore shall they eat of the fruit of their own way, and be filled with their own devices.

For the turning away of the simple shall slay them. And the prosperity of fools shall destroy them.

AMP 1:31.32   Therefore shall they eat of the fruit of their own way and be satiated with their own devices. For the backsliding of the simple shall slay them, and the careless ease of [self-confident] fools shall destroy them.

The "simples'" own unpredictable and unexpected inclinations will kill them and "fools" feeling satisfied with being unaware of actual dangers will destroy them.

Proverbs 9:12

NIV 9:12   If you are wise, your wisdom will reward you; if you are a mocker, you alone will suffer.

KJV 9:12   If thou be wise, thou shalt be wise for thyself: but if thou scornest, thou alone shalt bear it.

AMP 9:12   If you are wise, you are wise for yourself; if you scorn, you alone will bear it and pay the penalty.

If you are wise, that is, if you have become wise, your wisdom that you have will benefit you in all areas of life. Every decision you make will be made with discretion. The results of one wise decision after another, over a period of time, will provide you with blessings. If you "despise" wisdom, you will be the one to suffer the consequences. The word "despise" means an abrupt rejection or dismissal, to regard as negligible or unimportant.

3. They Will Make Their Parents Sad and Disappointed

NIV 10:1   The proverbs of Solomon: A wise son brings joy to his father, but a foolish son grief to his mother.

KJV 10:1   The proverbs of Solomon. A wise son maketh a glad father: but a foolish son is the heaviness of his mother.

AMP 10:1   The Proverbs of Solomon: A wise son makes a glad father, but a foolish and self-confident son is the grief of his mother.

A child who remains foolish as he or she grows up makes his or her parents sad and disappointed.

4. It Will Bring Shame Upon Them

NIV 14:35   A king delights in a wise servant, but a shameful servant incurs his wrath.

KJV 14:35   The king's favour is toward a wise servant: but his wrath is against him that causeth shame.

AMP 14:35   The king's favor is toward a wise and discreet servant, but his wrath is against him who does shamefully.

The word "king" here means one who holds a preeminent position, that is, having paramount rank, dignity or importance. In the days the Old Testament was written, there were kings, such as King Solomon, who wrote this verse, who had servants they owned who served them. Some were wiser than others. A "wise" servant pleased the king with his ability to discern inner qualities and relationships, knowledge, insight, good sense, good judgment, a wise attitude or course of action. However, a "shameful" servant will incur the king's "wrath." Shame is a condition of humiliating disgrace or brings strong regret. "Wrath" here means anger leading to punishment for an offense or crime, divine chastisement. The word "king" can represent God or Jesus Christ and the word "servant" can represent all born-again Christians today.

5. It Will Cause Their Family To Be Divided

NIV 14:1   The wise woman builds her house, but with her own hands the foolish one tears hers down.

KJV 14:1   Every wise woman buildeth her house: but the foolish plucketh it down with her hands.

AMP 14:1   Every wise woman builds her house, but the foolish one tears it down with her own hands.

The foolish woman, that is, the woman who lacks sound judgment, prudence and understanding, will cause her family and home to become separated or divided with her own actions and words.

6. Their Foolish Words Will Bring Them Punishment

NIV 14:3   A fool's talk brings a rod to his back, but the lips of the wise protect them.

KJV 14:3   In the mouth of the foolish is a rod of pride: but the lips of the wise shall preserve them.

AMP 14:3   In the fool's own mouth is a rod [to shame] his pride, but the wise men's lips preserve them.

"Pride" here suggests an assumed superiority or loftiness, even being arrogant, which implies a claiming for oneself of more consideration or importance than is warranted. In other words, thinking more highly of oneself than they should. A "rod" was a straight, slender stick or a bundle of twigs used to punish. The "foolish" person is one who lacks good judgment, prudence and understanding. Therefore, the foolish person will be punished because of the prideful, arrogant words that he speaks. However, the words of the wise will protect them, keeping them safe from injury, harm or destruction.

7. Leads to a Very Costly Undertaking

NIV 12:8   A man is praised according to his wisdom, but men with warped minds are despised.

KJV 12:8   A man shall be commended according to his wisdom: but he that is of a perverse heart shall be despised.

AMP 12:8   A man shall be commended according to his Wisdom [godly Wisdom, which is comprehensive insight into the ways and purposes of God], but he who is of a perverse heart shall be despised.

A person will be complimented and praised according to how much wisdom he or she has, but the person whose heart has turned away from what is right or good will be despised or strongly disliked.

Proverbs 14:24

NIV 14:24   The wealth of the wise is their crown, but the folly of fools yields folly.

KJV 14:24   The crown of the wise is their riches: but the foolishness of fools is folly.

AMP 14:24   The crown of the wise is their wealth of Wisdom, but the foolishness of [self-confident] fools is [nothing but] folly.

A "crown" is a reward of victory or mark of honor. Therefore, the reward of victory or mark of honor of the wise person is their wealth. "Foolishness" implies the character of being or seeming unable to use good judgment, discretion or good sense. "Fools" are people who lack good judgment, prudence and understanding. "Folly" here means an excessively costly or unprofitable undertaking. Therefore, "foolishness" or being unable to use good judgment, discretion or good sense, of people who lack good judgment, prudence and understanding, will lead to an excessively costly or unprofitable undertaking.

8. It Will Cost Them Financially

NIV 17:2   A wise servant will rule over a disgraceful son, and will share the inheritance as one of the brothers.

KJV 17:2   A wise servant shall have rule over a son that causeth shame, and shall have part of the inheritance among the brethren.

AMP 17:2   A wise servant shall have rule over a son who causes shame, and shall share in the inheritance among the brothers.

A wise servant, that is, a person who performs duties for the person or around the home of a master or personal employer, who does so by using good, sound judgment, keen discernment and deep understanding will have authority or control over a son who causes shame, something that brings humiliating disgrace and strong regret, to his parents. Not only will the wise servant rule over the son who brings shame, but he will also share in the inheritance along with the children. He will gain favor by doing his work well with a humble attitude.

9. They Will Become a Servant to the Wise

NIV 11:29 He who brings trouble on his family will inherit only wind, and the fool will be servant to the wise.

KJV 11:29 He that troubleth his own house shall inherit the wind: and the fool shall be servant to the wise of heart.

AMP 11:29 He who troubles his own house shall inherit the wind, and the foolish shall be servant to the wise of heart.

A person who "troubles" his own family shall inherit nothing. The word "trouble" means to agitate mentally or spiritually, to cause worry or to disturb. The fool, a person lacking in good judgment, prudence and understanding, will be "servant," which means one who performs duties about the person or home of a master or personal employer, to the wise of heart.

10. They Will Suffer Ruin, Defeat and Failure

NIV 10:8 The wise in heart accept commands, but a chattering fool comes to ruin.

KJV 10:8 The wise in heart will receive commandments: but a prating fool shall fall.

AMP 10:8   The wise in heart will accept and obey com-
           mandments, but the foolish of lips will fall
           headlong.

The person who is wise in their heart and wants to become
wiser is willing to listen to commands or instruction from others; they are teachable. But a fool, a person lacking in good
judgment, prudence and understanding, who talks a lot without really saying much, just chattering, will suffer ruin, defeat
and failure.

11. Destruction Will Come Upon Them

NIV 8:36   But whoever fails to find me harms himself;
           all who hate me love death.

KJV 8:36   But he that sinneth against me wrongeth his
           own soul: all they that hate me love death.

AMP 8:36   But he who misses me or sins against me
           wrongs and injures himself; all who hate me
           love and court death.

Whoever does not find wisdom or refuses to follow wisdom's
ways, only hurts himself (his own soul). If someone hates wisdom and refuses to listen to wisdom, destruction will come upon
him or her without them even realizing it.

I. Characteristics of Not Having Wisdom

1. Refuses to Accept Wisdom

NIV 8:3   beside the gates leading into the city, at the
           entrances, she cries aloud:

KJV 8:3   She crieth at the gates, at the entry of the city, at the coming in at the doors.

AMP 8:3   At the gates at the entrance of the town, at the coming in at the doors, she cries out:

Wisdom is "heard" by all people. However, many choose not to accept what they have heard.

Proverbs 9:12

NIV 9:12   If you are wise, your wisdom will reward you; if you are a mocker, you alone will suffer.

KJV 9:12   If thou be wise, thou shalt be wise for thyself: but if thou scornest, thou alone shalt bear it.

AMP 9:12   If you are wise, you are wise for yourself; if you scorn, you alone will bear it and pay the penalty.

If you are wise, that is, if you have become wise, your wisdom that you have will benefit you in all areas of life. Every decision you make will be made with discretion. The results of one wise decision after another, over a period of time, will provide you with blessings. If you "despise" wisdom, you will be the one to suffer the consequences. The word "despise" means an abrupt rejection or dismissal, to regard as negligible or unimportant.

2. Fools Hate Wisdom and Discipline

NIV 1:7   The fear of the Lord is the beginning of knowledge, but fools despise wisdom and discipline.

KJV 1:7   The fear of the LORD is the beginning of
            knowledge: but fools despise wisdom and in-
            struction.

AMP 1:7   The reverent and worshipful fear of the Lord
            is the beginning and the principal and choice
            part of knowledge [its starting point and its
            essence]; but fools despise skillful and godly
            Wisdom, instruction, and discipline.

Fools, or people lacking good judgment or common sense,
strongly dislike wisdom and discipline.

3. Ignores Widsom and Has No Desire to Have Knowledge

NIV 1:20   Wisdom calls aloud in the street, she raises her
            voice in the public squares;

KJV 1:20   Wisdom crieth without; she uttereth her voice
            in the streets:

AMP 1:20 Wisdom cries aloud in the street, she raises her
            voice in the markets;

The "simple" people, or those who seem unable or unwilling to use good judgment and make responsible decisions, continue their simple ways. "Mockers," or those who ridicule others with insulting words or actions, continue to ridicule others.

NIV 1:21   at the head of the noisy streets she cries out,
            in the gateways of the city she makes her
            speech:

KJV 1:21   She crieth in the chief place of concourse, in

the openings of the gates: in the city she uttereth her words, saying,

AMP 1:21 She cries at the head of the noisy intersections
[in the chief gathering places]; at the entrance
of the city gates she speaks:

Fools, people who lack good judgment or common sense,
do not care about having knowledge.

4. Reasons Why Some People Do Not Have Wisdom

NIV 8:2 On the heights along the way, where the paths
meet, she takes her stand;

KJV 8:2 She standeth in the top of high places, by the
way in the places of the paths.

AMP 8:2 On the top of the heights beside the way,
where the paths meet, stands Wisdom [skill-
ful and godly];

Wisdom and understanding are very visible; they cannot be
missed. They are clearly evident to everyone. Again, people's
poor decisions and choices are the reasons why they do not
have wisdom and understanding. They decide or choose not to
spend time in God's Word.

5. He Has No Desire to Get Wisdom

NIV 17:16 Of what use is money in the hand of a fool,
since he has no desire to get wisdom?

KJV 17:16 Wherefore is there a price in the hand of a fool
to get wisdom, seeing he hath no heart to it?

AMP 17:16　Of what use is money in the hand of a [self-confident] fool to buy skillful and godly Wisdom–when he has no understanding or heart for it?

A fool does not care about wisdom. Regardless of how much money someone pays a fool to get wisdom, if his heart is not set on getting wisdom, he will not obtain it.

6. Fools Will Not Listen to Others

NIV 12:15　The way of a fool seems right to him, but a wise man listens to advice.

KJV 12:15　The way of a fool is right in his own eyes: but he that hearkeneth unto counsel is wise.

AMP 12:15　The way of a fool is right in his own eyes, but he who listens to counsel is wise.

The fool, that is, the person lacking in sound judgment, prudence and understanding, always thinks he is right and will not listen to others. He will argue to try to prove his point.

7. They Will Not Listen When Rebuked

NIV 13:1　A wise son heeds his father's instruction, but a mocker does not listen to rebuke.

KJV 13:1　A wise son heareth his father's instruction: but a scorner heareth not rebuke.

AMP 13:1　A wise son heeds [and is the fruit of] his father's instruction and correction, but a scoffer listens not to rebuke.

A scorner, that is, a person who despises and displays open dislike and disrespect for something or someone, will not listen when he is rebuked or criticized sharply.

8. Resents Someone Correcting Him

NIV 15:12   A mocker resents correction; he will not consult the wise.

KJV 15:12   A scorner loveth not one that reproveth him: neither will he go unto the wise.

AMP 15:12 A scorner has no love for one who rebukes him; neither will he go to the wise [for counsel].

A person who treats others with contempt, that is, he despises and has no respect for others, who ridicules others with insulting actions or words, resents someone correcting him. He is stubborn and refuses to listen to wise people.

9. Displays Violent and Uncontrollable Anger

NIV 14:16   A wise man fears the LORD and shuns evil, but a fool is hotheaded and reckless.

KJV 14:16   A wise man feareth, and departeth from evil: but the fool rageth, and is confident.

AMP 14:16   A wise man suspects danger and cautiously avoids evil, but the fool bears himself insolently and is [presumptuously] confident.

The fool displays violent and uncontrollable anger. Talking to him will do no good, as he is determined that his opinion or what he is angry about is right. This behavior will only get him into more trouble.

NIV 29:8   Mockers stir up a city, but wise men turn away anger.

KJV 29:8   Scornful men bring a city into a snare: but wise men turn away wrath.

AMP 29:8   Scoffers set a city afire [inflaming the minds of the people], but wise men turn away wrath.

People who have open dislike and disrespect for others, treating others with ridicule and insulting action or speech, bring the people of the city into a "trap," entangling them in difficulties.

Proverbs 29:11

NIV 29:11   A fool gives full vent to his anger, but a wise man keeps himself under control.

KJV 29:11   A fool uttereth all his mind: but a wise man keepeth it in till afterwards.

AMP 29:11   A [self-confident] fool utters all his anger, but a wise man holds it back and stills it.

A foolish person speaks whatever comes to his mind before thinking about what he is saying. When anger arises, the foolish person reacts in anger, making the situation even worse. However, a wise person controls his anger and restrains himself from saying something that would cause even more anger.

10. Speaks Words That Are Absurd, Ridiculous and Based on Poor Judgment

NIV 15:2   The tongue of the wise commends knowledge, but the mouth of the fool gushes folly.

KJV 15:2   The tongue of the wise useth knowledge aright: but the mouth of fools poureth out foolishness.

AMP 15:2   The tongue of the wise utters knowledge rightly, but the mouth of the [self-confident] fool pours out folly.

The wise person speaks words from his knowledge correctly, which means to help and give good advice to other people. But the words of fools, people who lack good judgment, prudence and understanding, are foolishness, or are ideas that are absurd, ridiculous and based on poor judgment.

11. Speaks Destructive Words

NIV 10:14   Wise men store up knowledge, but the mouth of a fool invites ruin.

KJV 10:14   Wise men lay up knowledge: but the mouth of the foolish is near destruction.

AMP 10:14   Wise men store up knowledge [in mind and heart], but the mouth of the foolish is a present destruction.

The foolish person, that is, the person who is lacking in sound judgment or prudence and understanding, speaks words before he thinks and the words he speaks will cause destruction or ruin, destroying relationships. He never can remain silent. He is always talking.

12. His Words Do Not Distribute Knowledge

NIV 15:7   The lips of the wise spread knowledge; not so the hearts of fools.

KJV 15:7   The lips of the wise disperse knowledge: but the heart of the foolish doeth not so.

AMP 15:7   The lips of the wise disperse knowledge [sifting it as chaff from the grain]; not so the minds and hearts of the self-confident and foolish.

The foolish person does not have wisdom; therefore, his words do not distribute knowledge.

13. Excuses

NIV 30:24   Four things on earth are small, yet they are extremely wise:

KJV 30:24   There be four things which are little upon the earth, but they are exceeding wise:

AMP 30:24   There are four things which are little on the earth, but they are exceedingly wise:

"Excuses" are being addressed here. People often use excuses why they are not prosperous, not successful, not liked, not happy, etc. Four creatures on the earth are used to illustrate that although a person may not possess certain attributes, it does not mean that they cannot have an exceptional amount, quality or degree of wisdom.

14. Spends All of His Money as He Gets It

NIV 21:20   In the house of the wise are stores of choice

food and oil, but a foolish man devours all he has.

KJV 21:20   There is treasure to be desired and oil in the dwelling of the wise; but a foolish man spendeth it up.

AMP 21:20   There are precious treasures and oil in the dwelling of the wise, but a self-confident and foolish man swallows it up and wastes it.

A wise person invests his money wisely and does not spend it frivolously. Therefore, he will be prosperous and have money in reserve. However, a foolish person, that is, a person who lacks good judgment and common sense, spends all of his money as he gets it.

15. Is Deceived of the Effects Alcohol Has on Them

NIV 20:1   Wine is a mocker and beer a brawler; whoever is led astray by them is not wise.

KJV 20:1   Wine is a mocker, strong drink is raging: and whosoever is deceived thereby is not wise.

AMP 20:1   Wine is a mocker, strong drink a riotous brawler; and whoever errs or reels because of it is not wise.

The person who does not realize that wine will cause a person to treat others with contempt or ridicule with insulting words or actions and that alcohol will cause a person to treat others with violent and uncontrollable anger, is deceived. That is, he or she accepting something as true, which is false. They are not wise.

16. Does Not Like Their Mother

NIV 15:20 A wise son brings joy to his father, but a foolish man despises his mother.

KJV 15:20 A wise son maketh a glad father: but a foolish man despiseth his mother.

AMP 15:20 A wise son makes a glad father, but a self-confident and foolish man despises his mother and puts her to shame.

A foolish man looks down on his mother with contempt, regards her as worthless, has a strong dislike for her and rejects her.

17. They Can Learn to Become Wiser

NIV 21:11 When a mocker is punished, the simple gain wisdom; when a wise man is instructed, he gets knowledge.

KJV 21:11 When the scorner is punished, the simple is made wise: and when the wise is instructed, he receiveth knowledge.

AMP 21:11 When the scoffer is punished, the fool gets a lesson in being wise; but men of [godly] Wisdom and good sense learn by being instructed.

When the scorner, a person who openly shows dislike, disrespect and contempt, is punished, the simple, that is, the person who is unable to use sound judgment, discretion or good sense, is made wise or learns from it.

CONCLUSION

Now that you have read this book, what do you do next to obtain Knowledge, Understanding and Wisdom?

First, go back through and read, meditate and study until you grasp not only the Knowledge, but also thorough understanding of all aspects of Knowledge, Understanding and Wisdom. Reviewing the table of contents will help you to see the "whole picture."

Review Chapter 4 under Wisdom, "How to Get Wisdom," Chapter 5, "Characteristics of Having Wisdom," Chapter 6, "Wisdom's Instruction to Us" and Chapter 7, "What Having Wisdom Will Do for You," envisioning you getting wisdom, having wisdom, doing what wisdom instructs you to do, and enjoying all that Wisdom will do for you.

Second, pray to God, asking Him to reveal to you the Understanding and to give you Wisdom as you "seek after" His Knowledge, Understanding and Wisdom.

Ask Him for guidance and direction every day. Pray that every decision that you make will be based on wisdom and that you will use discretion and discernment. Pray in the Holy Spirit to sensitize yourself to "hear" what God is wanting to say to you, through the Holy Spirit that lives in your heart. Understand that your mind and your spirit are interlinked, they communicate. This is how God can get ideas, answers and insight to your mind, through the Holy Spirit. The Holy Spirit is our Helper. That is His job. However, He can only help us if we listen to His instruction and obey. We must learn to recognize His "voice" and act upon it. First step is to recognize His voice or prompting. Second step is to choose to obey, do what He says to do.

Now, you have a choice to make. The choice, without a doubt, will affect the rest of your life. Here is the choice: Do you only read this book for informational purposes and do nothing more? If so, it will not provide you with all the benefits of having Wisdom. Or, will you read, study and meditate with a burning desire to obtain the Knowledge, Understanding and Wisdom that God wants you to have? If you will, I assure you God will perform His Word. He will reveal His Understanding to you and give you Wisdom that will greatly bless you in every area of your life!

As you read and study God's Word and pray, He will give you Wisdom in all areas of life: finances, family, relationships, business and much more. You are probably wondering, *How does God give me Wisdom in all these other areas when I am spending my time in His Word and praying? That doesn't make sense to my human mind*, you're thinking. Here's the simple answer: It doesn't have to! God is only looking for our trust in Him and our obedience. If we do what He has instructed and commanded us to do, He will fulfill His promises! Let's do our part and allow God to bless us with all the benefits of having His Wisdom!

May God bless you as you begin Living the Wisdom of Solomon!

Testimony
John W. Pride

I was raised in the state of Kentucky. I grew up playing basketball. As a high school senior I was recruited to play basketball in college. The decision I had before me at the age of eighteen was whether or not to play basketball at the University of Evansville in Indiana—located only an hour's drive from where I lived. Because of this, I knew many of my family, friends and my girlfriend would be able to come see me play. As you can see, there were plenty of good reasons to attend the University of Evansville. However, there was another choice I had to consider. And while it meant I would be attending school more than six hundred miles from home, the invitation was on the table from Oral Roberts University in Tulsa, Oklahoma.

In the natural, there were strong advantages to staying close to home. However, I knew there was a "right" decision and I knew how to get to it... I prayed. After praying and consulting the Holy Spirit, it became clear to me that I should go to Oral Roberts University. As I worked through my own personal questions about the decision I was making, there was a peace in my spirit when I thought about going to Oral Roberts University.

The decision made, in the summer of 1977, I moved to Tulsa, Oklahoma, prepared to enroll and play basketball at ORU. Because basketball was very important to me, playing at the college level had been a dream of mine all my life. And because of that dream, there was an excitement that began to stir as I drove on the campus of ORU.

However, it didn't take long for me to learn that an unexpected event was taking place as I was traveling to Tulsa. The head basketball coach, the same coach who recruited me to play at ORU, lost his job! As that first day progressed, I learned there was more unsettling news. In addition to learning that the new basketball coach was bringing his recruits with him, I also learned there were no more scholarship positions left on the team.

Hurt and disappointed, I began to question whether or not I had missed God's leading through the Holy Spirit. I didn't think so. And while I simply had no explanation as to why this was happening to me, there was still a peace in my spirit about being at ORU. In the midst of all the questions, the hurt and the disappointment taking pace in my life, I knew I was exactly where God wanted me to be and I was doing exactly what He wanted me to be doing. With that assurance, I enrolled in Oral Roberts University, not as a basketball player, but as as a student, facing the disappointment of my freshman year sitting in the stands as the other guys played the game.

In December 1977—during my first semester at ORU—the University of Evansville's basketball team boarded a plane bound for an out-of-town game. In an attempt to take off in a rainstorm, their plane crashed, killing everyone on board!

As I heard the news of the crash I was shocked! And then the reality of what had happened to the players and coaches of the University of Evansville basketball team became very personal as I realized I could have been on that plane had I not followed the direction of the Holy Spirit.

It put things in perspective for me. I learned that following the guidance of the Holy Spirit could save my life!

From the experience of my walking out the choices as to where I was to play basketball, I learned the Holy Spirit—the "alongside one" lives inside me and is available for me every second of every day. I became personally aware of how He wants to help, teach, guide, comfort and counsel me. And from reading the Bible I knew God sent the Holy Spirit to be my Helper, plus I learned something more. I learned that helping us is His job, His assignment from God. However, in order for Him to help me...for Him to fulfill His assignment, it is up to me to ask Him for His help and it is up to me to be sensitive and responsive to His direction.

While the Holy Spirit may not "speak" to us in an audible voice, He does speak to those who will listen. He "speaks" through His peace in our spirit, an inner witness in our spirit. In addition to allowing us to experience His peace as a witness to His Spirit at work in our lives, He "speaks" to us by placing godly ideas, concepts and plans in our minds.

I tell you, on the authority of God's Word, the Holy Spirit can and wants to help you make the wisest decisions throughout every area of your life. Being led by the Spirit, coupled with operating in the wisdom God gives every believer who will receive and participate in His plan for their life, will bring success to every area of your life!

It is my prayer that you will allow the words of this book to both take root in your spirit and expand into every facet of your personal and professional life as you experience *Living the Wisdom of Solomon.*

To order additional copies:

John W. Pride
Post Office Box 702002
Tulsa, Oklahoma 74170-2002
Phone: 918-841-2867 Fax: 918-524-9292

Website: www.johnwpride.com

Email: johnwpride@cox.net